BOBBY BOWDEN ON LEADERSHIP

BOBBY BOWDEN ON LEADERSHIP

Life Lessons from a Two-Time
National Championship Coach

PAT WILLIAMS
with ROB WILSON

Published by Advantage, Charleston, South Carolina.
Member of Advantage Media Group.

ADVANTAGE is a registered trademark and the Advantage colophon is a trademark of Advantage Media Group, Inc.

Printed in the United States of America.

ISBN: 978-159932-264-3
LCCN: 2011939165

This publication is designed to provide accurate and authoritative information in regard to the subject matter covered. It is sold with the understanding that the publisher is not engaged in rendering legal, accounting, or other professional services. If legal advice or other expert assistance is required, the services of a competent professional person should be sought.

Credits:
Front Cover: Photo by: Mitchell White
Rear Cover: Photo by: Miguel A Olivella, Jr./BaselineShots Photography

Advantage Media Group is proud to be a part of the Tree Neutral™ program. Tree Neutral offsets the number of trees consumed in the production and printing of this book by taking proactive steps such as planting trees in direct proportion to the number of trees used to print books. To learn more about Tree Neutral, please visit www.treeneutral.com. To learn more about Advantage's commitment to being a responsible steward of the environment, please visit www.advantagefamily.com/green

Advantage Media Group is a leading publisher of business, motivation, and self-help authors. Do you have a manuscript or book idea that you would like to have considered for publication? Please visit www.amgbook.com or call 1.866.775.1696

*I dedicate this book to my dear friend and longtime business partner,
Jimmy Hewitt, who introduced me to the "magic" of Seminole football.*

- PAT WILLIAMS

*I dedicate this book to Sherrill, Preston and Parker, who remind
me every day to be a better person. And to my Dad, who would
have corrected my grammar, and then burst with pride.*

- ROB WILSON

CONTENTS

IT STARTED OVER LUNCH

Bobby Bowden on Leadership started with an interesting young man named Adam Witty. Witty grew up in my adopted home of Orlando, Florida and graduated from Clemson University. As a Wake Forest graduate, I have thus far managed not to hold that against him. He has many talents but above all of them might be his entrepreneurial spirit.

In his early '20s, Witty launched a publishing company in Charleston, South Carolina and would seek my counsel on occasion when it came to business decisions. Even though I'm 40 years older, we have common interests including sports, books and successful leadership models.

One day over lunch we began to talk leadership and coaching. It wasn't long before we were scribbling out a list of the best coaches that the sports world had produced. We agreed that the coaches we were interested in had to have had a lifetime of leadership success. It was an interesting discussion and generated a list that was not all that long. I looked up from my iced tea with extra mint and lemon and told Adam that I would be willing to write a book on one coach to get the experiment started if he would publish it. Adam agreed quickly and over two desserts we talked long into the afternoon about who should be the first case study.

It turned out to be Bear Bryant – the legendary Alabama football coach. And so I spent the summer of 2010 immersed in the life of Paul Bryant. However, the book never would have happened without the help of Tommy Ford. A member of the University of Alabama athletic department, he is constantly in touch with former Alabama players and all things Crimson Tide. He would become my writing partner on *Bear Bryant on Leadership* and a skilled one at that.

Our Bryant book was released in November 2010 and received wide acclaim and was quite successful. The book got many compliments from former players and we felt really good about the project.

Adam then came to me grinning, "Who's next?" he asked. The question led to another long discussion as we marveled at the accomplishments of Joe Paterno and Tom Osborne and Woody Hayes and Bo Schembechler and Mike Krzyzewski and Pat Summitt. I eliminated UCLA basketball legend John Wooden since I had already written two books about him and felt I had exhausted my capacity to write anything more about the greatest coach of all time.

"I think the next leader we examine is Bobby Bowden," I proclaimed.

Now, Adam likes to challenge people, so he simply asked, "Why?"

"His career is all over the record book," I began. "He is easy to promote and interesting to college fans all over the country." Adam nodded in quick agreement and asked how long I would need.

My next thought was, "I've got to find the Tommy Ford of Florida State," which proved easier than I imagined.

While in Tuscaloosa to promote the Bryant book, I ran into Nick Saban's publicist who, as it turned out, had come from Florida State via the Orange Bowl. "Rob Wilson" was Jeff Purinton's quick and emphatic answer to my question on who could help me tell the Bowden story. "Rob will know where the players and the stories are; just relax and call him."

I dialed Rob up sight unseen and pitched my idea. "You can count on me," he said with a remarkable lack of hesitation or reservation. My kind of guy.

Our research began and we quickly began to trace Bobby Bowden from his first coaching jobs at South Georgia College and then his alma mater Howard College (now Samford University). We got unbelievable cooperation with folks from these early stops only to be exceeded by the gracious and enthusiastic response from those with ties to Bowden during his coaching career at West Virginia. We dug up just about every former Seminole we could find in a massive effort that included interviewing over 300 people for the book.

I would do the interviews and would reach out to former players from these four schools, as well as former coaches, administrators and opposing coaches with one simple question. "What made Bobby Bowden a good leader?" I might follow with one or two questions about his strengths or what he did, but that was about it.

Needless to say I raced through multiple legal pads of quotes from interview subjects as old as 90 and as young as 21. And in all those interviews I never heard one negative comment. Not one disgruntled player and apparently not one out there holding a grudge. I never even had one player who did not want to talk.

Remarkable.

You're in for a valuable and informative reading experience! You are going to want to have a pen with you at all times. You are going to be circling things, bending pages and copying quotes. Above all please take the principles and observations about this great leader and apply them to your life. Our nation is in desperate need of leadership. We are starved as a society today for strong leaders who have the courage of their convictions. The nation wants and needs people strong enough to do what is right no matter what backlash follows. Political affiliation, religious affiliation, race, economic status, all of those things matter, but none of them should prevent our nation from following the right path. Somewhere along the line doing what is right, good and proper has become an attack on personal freedoms. Only strong leadership can steer our nation back on track.

I have spent a lifetime studying and teaching on the subject of leadership. I am convinced and have defended my convictions in many a venue that you can take any great leader throughout history and they will possess the same Seven Dimensions of Leadership. Historical figures as seemingly unrelated as Jesus Christ, Winston Churchill and Bear Bryant tie their successful leadership qualities back to these fundamentals. Your favorite teacher, or coach, or boss likely has the same attributes. A great leader possesses Vision, Communication Skills, People Skills, Character, Competence, Boldness and a Serving Heart. There are layers and layers underneath these qualities to be sure, but great leadership is born of these seven essentials.

I think you will find that Bowden, just as Bear Bryant and every other great leader in history, displays the seven leadership qualities that I studied and identified years ago. It does not matter what place in history or what field the leader is in, they will fall perfectly into these seven leadership principles.

The hope Rob and I have with this book is that you will take the qualities that Bobby Bowden used to become such a successful leader and apply them in your life. You are a leader. You are a leader in your home, your church, your work, your little league park, your community, your nation – so don't wait – learn how Bobby Bowden's principles can work for you.

Rob told me early on in this process that, "Bobby Bowden is the best man that I have ever met." Now after writing this book, I would add he was as good a leader as you will ever meet.

Get ready for a powerful reading experience.

THE SEVEN SIDES OF LEADERSHIP

Leadership has become a gigantic industry unto itself in our country. Hardly a week goes by that I don't get another brochure or mailing piece about a leadership conference or seminar or retreat. And that doesn't take into account the books that are pouring out on leadership, seemingly by the day.

I think it all started in 1992 when a man named Donald T. Phillips wrote a book called *Lincoln on Leadership*. He spent years trying to get it published and the publishers told him that the problem is that there's just no place to put it in the bookstores; there's just no category on "leadership." So he was turned down many times.

Finally the book was published and it became a huge success, and an industry was launched in the publishing world. Then a pastor on the west coast, John Maxwell, wrote a book called *The 21 Irrefutable Laws of Leadership*. It hit the *New York Times* bestseller list and the barn door was open at that point. Now, leadership books are coming out in droves.

And, many of them are built around people – many of the biblical personalities have books about them. We have David on leadership and Jesus on leadership and Moses on leadership, including one book called *Moses on Management*. And then there are the Civil War personalities – you can read about Robert E. Lee on leadership and Ulysses S. Grant on leadership, and when you get to World War II, the books are abounding – from Truman on leadership to Eisenhower on leadership

to Roosevelt, to Churchill, to General Patton, to General Marshall…
it just never ends.

And you can't be in the sports business unless you've written your
book on leadership. We have Pat Summitt on leadership and Mike
Krzyzewski on leadership and Joe Torre on leadership and Lou Holtz
on leadership and even – Bobby Bowden on leadership and on and on.

But I wanted to hear a few words from Bear Bryant on leadership.
I wished that Coach Bryant had written in depth on the topic, but
he passed away in 1983. I felt certain that Bryant had a message and
advice for leaders both today and in the future.

So I set about writing a book with the help of Alabama expert
Tommy Ford that might convey the principles and practices of the
great Bear Bryant. It was an eye-opening experience. The book *Bear
Bryant On Leadership* was a commercial success, but even more than
that I think we were able to assemble a fantastic resource from the
accounts of the players who played for him, the coaches who coached
both for and against him, and the many others whose lives he touched.

The very next great in the sports world that I wanted to hear from
was Bobby Bowden and I felt as though I had really hit on a special
book after hearing from those he led. I am so proud that we have
launched this project with Advantage Media Group. The research into
for book has been vast and in-depth. With the enthusiastic assistance of
both the West Virginia and Florida State Athletic Departments and my
writing partner Rob Wilson, I've been able to track down 300 people
who knew Coach Bowden. Through my interviews with them we have
brought into clear focus all of Coach Bowden's leadership principles.

I am a fanatic on the subject of leadership. I have bought most of
the leadership books over the years; as a matter of fact, I have almost
700 leadership books perched in my leadership library at home. In
addition to that, I have spent 53 years at the highest level of college

and professional athletics, the last 43 as an executive in the National Basketball Association.

Through all of my study, I came away convinced that to be a leader for the ages, a leader who makes an enormous impact, there are seven qualities or sides of leadership that must be in place. With all due apologies to my good friend John Maxwell and his *21 Irrefutable Laws of Leadership,* this book is designed to focus on these seven sides of leadership that I have discovered all great leaders possess, and match it up with what Coach Bowden did for over 50 years in college football as a leader. The more I studied Bowden as a leader and the more interviews I conducted, the more convinced I became that he truly was a seven-sided leader.

As you read the reflections and the teaching points that come from all of these people who knew him well, the mission of this book is to make you a better leader. Whether you're leading in education, the military, the church, athletics, business, or the highest levels of government, this book is designed to help you discover the keys to being a seven-sided leader through the life of college football legend Bobby Bowden.

Sit down and get ready for a read that could change your life. Make sure to take notes and I hope you end up circling and writing all over this book. I drove by a church once and the marquee read, "The person's whose Bible is tattered, usually has a life that's not."

BOBBY BOWDEN

Bobby Bowden knew the challenge when he became Florida State's head coach in 1976. "When I was at Alabama, their bumper stickers read '*Beat Auburn*'. When I was at West Virginia the bumper stickers said '*Beat Pitt*'. When I got the job at FSU, they had bumper stickers that read '*Beat Anybody*.'"

The quote made the lead of virtually every story written from that introductory press conference at FSU which launched a most remarkable 34 years in Tallahassee. During those years, Bowden proved he was up for that and every other challenge over a career that eventually would include more wins, 388, than all but Penn State's Joe Paterno in college football history. His success with the Seminoles includes winning unanimous National Championships in 1993 and 1999.

For 14 seasons from 1987 to 2001, Bowden's Seminole teams never finished outside of the Associated Press Top 5. No college football program has ever been that consistently outstanding and one struggles to find a parallel anywhere in the sporting world. What would a basketball program that reached the NCAA Final Four for 14 straight years be considered?

To put just these two Bowden achievements in perspective consider what it would take for his successor at Florida State, or any other second year coach for that matter, to overtake him. All he would have to do is win 10 games next season and do that for the next 31 years. Whew!

Bowden was half joking with FSU fans when he came on board, but the dire condition of the program that he pulled and pushed to the top of the college football world was no joke. Bowden had to rebuild everything at Florida State all the way down to designing the now familiar helmets and helping round up a horse to start the Osceola and Renegade tradition.

He earned the nickname "Riverboat Gambler" for his wide open offensive style at both West Virginia and FSU that included running his favorite play, the "reverse," at unconventional times, as well as having a pocket full of trick plays ready to go for every game, along with the courage to call them.

Popular today as a speaker both on his Christian faith and coaching values, Bowden's self-deprecating style and approachable nature served him extremely well as this book should attest, but some note that those qualities may also have masked the fierce competitiveness, coaching genius and skilled leadership qualities that are as much a part of his makeup as his easy smile.

Born in Birmingham, Alabama, in 1929, Robert Cleckler Bowden's father, Bob Bowden, was a teller at First National Bank in Birmingham and described by Bobby as a "big football fan." His mother, Sunset, was a homemaker and he had one sister, Marion, who was 18 months his elder.

The home the Bowdens lived in until Bobby reached age five may have had more impact on sports history than we know since it was located less than first down yardage from the football fields of Woodlawn High. A young Bowden could hear the sounds of football from just over the hedge and it was not long before his father would pull his young son onto the roof to watch the Woodlawn players go through practice after practice.

Born to Coach is how author Mark Schlabach titled his outstanding book on Bowden – one that makes my list of ten most influential books by the way – and those three words perfectly crystallize how Bowden feels about his career calling. You don't have to spend a lot of time researching or interviewing people about Bobby Bowden before realizing that coaching seemed to him to almost be predestined, assuming a deeply rooted Baptist can borrow a bit from the Presbyterians.

The Bowden family, as was the case with nearly every American, was dramatically impacted by the trying times of the Great Depression. While the Bowdens were perhaps more insulated than some families, since his father never lost his job, Bowden's grandfather did have to give up a thriving business building courthouses. He would move in with the Bowden family and even share a cramped room with Bobby, an experience he would never forget.

Just before Bowden turned six, the family moved to another three bedroom Birmingham home, which, coincidentally, was within a block of Berry Field at Howard College (now Samford University). Bowden now spent afternoons watching Howard College practice as well as going with his dad to high school games at fabled Legion Field in Birmingham.

Bowden has hinted through countless interviews over his career that he was no less mischievous than any youngster growing up. He is quick to dispel any suggestion that he was the perfect child, even doing so from the pulpit to this day. The difference, he suggested to the late Bill McGrotha in the *Tallahassee Democrat*, was that shooting out streetlights with a BB gun or chucking stolen peaches from a neighbor's tree was considered pretty rough behavior in those days.

The flying peaches and shattering glass sound like modest offenses today, but Bowden is convinced that his exuberant spirit helped him understand young people over the next 70 years.

Sports, and football in particular, filled the daydreams of a young Bowden who was making a name for himself in YMCA sports as well as neighborhood pickup games. But all that seemed to come crashing down just as he was coming into his own.

As a 13-year-old in 1943, Bowden came home from a YMCA basketball game with swollen, painful legs. His mother drove him to the doctor's office where a diagnosis was made that Bowden remembers "had my mom crying all the way home." Rheumatic fever, a potentially fatal disease in the 1940s, was crushing news. Bowden was immediately confined to bed for the next year of his life with a doctor making a daily house call to "jab a needle in my arm." Bowden was in intense pain at times during his illness and doctors told his family that he would never play football. In fact, his parents were cautioned that he must never do anything stressful if he wanted to live past 40.

Bowden needed something to occupy his time and his mind as he lay there. Of course there was no TV in those days, but there was radio and all things World War II became his steady companion during the illness. Edward R. Murrow and other legendary correspondents would hold his attention for hours every day as reports from the battlefronts crackled across the radio. Bowden developed a mental map of the numerous theatres and knew where most of the military units were at any given time and which generals were leading them.

When he was not listening to the war and filling a drawing pad with sketches of war planes, ships and military weapons – which he still has to this day – he listened to college football games. His love of the University of Alabama was a natural, given that Tuscaloosa was right down the road, and he listened to every game they played. But when he couldn't hear the Tide games he would tune in to follow Auburn or any other game he could catch.

Bowden would recover from rheumatic fever, but escaping the shadow of the initial gloomy prognosis would prove harder. Doctors refused to let him play football so he played trombone in the Woodlawn marching band for two years just to be a part of the game he loved so much. Eventually, he convinced his parents to visit a cardiologist who pronounced him healthy enough to play.

At 5'5" and 115 pounds, Bowden was small when he first went out for football at Woodlawn, the same high school his home backed up to as a youngster. However, by his junior year he had grown in both physical stature and ability. He played running back and was co-captain of the 1948 team.

Something else happened during his junior year – he met Ann Estock. Bowden still describes Ann, his wife of over 55 years, as "the prettiest girl anybody ever saw," and the two would be a couple or, better put, a team from 1947 to this day.

After high school graduation in 1949, Bowden headed to Tusca-loosa to play football for his beloved Crimson Tide. He lasted only one semester, admitting to being completely homesick for Birmingham although it was just 45 miles away. He couldn't live without Ann. The two snuck over to Georgia and got married on April 1, 1949. Bobby was 19 and Ann 16. The secret did not last long and so the young couple moved in with his parents and enrolled at Howard College.

Bowden hit the football field and quickly showed his ability. The coaches moved him from running back to quarterback in 1950 and he would make Little All-American as a senior in 1954. Along the way, their first child Robyn was born in 1951 and son Steve arrived the next year. Thanks to living with her in-laws, Ann was able to attend Howard, join a sorority and even became a cheerleader with two babies at home.

College football was everything Bowden dreamed it would be and more. He earned a reputation as a tenacious player with complete control of the huddle and a penchant for changing a play, much to the surprise of his coaches.

Bowden would stay and coach at Howard for three years after graduating and earn a master's degree from Peabody College. The growing young family added Tommy in 1954, and Bowden got his first head coaching job at the age of 29 at South Georgia College. Just two years later, he returned to Howard College as head coach.

He would coach Howard for four seasons, posting a 31-6 record, including a 9-1 finish in his first season that put his career on the fast track. Bowden developed a relationship with Bear Bryant while an assistant at Howard and the legendary Alabama coach would send three to four players a year from his full-to-the-brim squads to Bobby, which helped his squad immensely.

In 1963, the Bowdens got itchy for a bigger and better paying job. While Howard and Birmingham were comfortable, both Bowdens admit it was Ann's encouragement that convinced Bobby to start climbing the coaching ladder. As fate would have it, the next rung was in Tallahassee where head coach Bill Peterson, considered one of the top offensive minds in football, needed a receivers coach. Longtime Bowden friend Vince Gibson coached the Seminole linebackers and convinced Peterson to hire Bowden.

Three years later, West Virginia had an opening for an offensive coordinator and the next rung of the ladder appeared. WVU head coach Jim Carlen was a defensive specialist who knew he had to hire a good offensive coach. "I was coming from Georgia Tech and coached defense. I told myself when I get to West Virginia, I've gotta find someone who knows the throwing game," he would tell the Lakeland Ledger.

Bowden took the reins of the Mountaineer offense that often lost the recruiting battles for the big lineman to nearby Pitt and Penn State, but generally had good talent at the skill positions. Three years later

Carlen left for Texas Tech and recommended the 40-year-old Bowden for the position.

Throughout this book you will learn more about the triumphs and challenges of Bowden's career mostly during his time with the Mountaineers and Seminoles and the leadership qualities he used to guide him through those times. But his WVU years alone were packed with all the highs and lows that come with high profile coaching. Bowden would coach the Mountaineers for six seasons from 1970-75. He led WVU to the Peach Bowl twice (1972, 1975) and posted a 42-26 record in Morgantown.

But a 1974 team that appeared on paper to be loaded with talent would dramatically underachieve and likely changed Bowden forever. Frustrated WVU fans hung Bowden in effigy, planted a For Sale sign in the front lawn of their home and hung bed sheets from dorm windows that begged the coach to leave. During this challenging time Bowden had two sons, Terry and Tommy, playing football for the Mountaineers and a family, that now included Jeff and Ginger, that had grown to love Morgantown.

Bowden and WVU rebounded the next season with a 9-3 record in 1975 that reignited the Mountaineer faithful, but also caught the attention of Florida State officials searching for a coach to rescue a floundering program.

Many FSU officials remembered Bowden from his previous stint and the important ones knew he had resurrected Howard from the football doldrums, but this was on a much bigger scale. Some might suggest that the hole was even deeper. Florida State had won just four games over the three seasons prior to 1976 and there was talk among the movers and shakers that perhaps FSU should consider dropping football.

BOBBY BOWDEN ON LEADERSHIP

Maryland's Jerry Claiborne seemed to be the hot name at the time for the FSU job, which made sense since his Terrapins had just beaten Florida in a bowl game. Apparently, the job didn't look the same from where Claiborne was sitting as he pulled his name out early. Behind the scenes, FSU President Stanley Marshall and Athletic Director Tom Bridgers had already decided on their man.

While there is no doubt that the For Sale sign made the Bowden's decision to leave the WVU job easier, there was also no premonition by Bobby or Ann that the rung they were now reaching would be their last and would take the Seminoles to the top of the college football world. In fact, Ann had a hard time with the move since it separated their close-knit family for the first time. Steve and Robyn had already left home, but Tommy and Terry would stay with the Mountaineer football team, while Jeff and Ginger would make the move to Tallahassee.

The rest of the story is college football history. Bowden would coach the Seminoles for the next 34 years (1976-2009) eventually becoming the second winningest coach in the history of college football. He coached 26 consensus All-Americans, won more bowl games than all but one other coach in history and took his Seminoles to 28 straight bowls. He did all this without changing his style or compromising his fundamental beliefs.

Bobby and Ann became known as the First Family of college football. Terry eventually became head coach of the Auburn Tigers and went undefeated in his first season. He is now head coach at North Alabama. Tommy became head coach at Tulane and Clemson and even coached four games against his father. Youngest son Jeff rose to offensive coordinator at FSU under his dad and now coaches at North Alabama as well. And the whole group has combined for 21 grandchildren and three great grandchildren – so far!

Bobby, meanwhile, is a better than average musician, I'm told his drawing skills are outstanding, he is an authority on World War II history, a dynamic believer in his God and a study in what balance, drive, priorities and faith can achieve.

"When I was thirteen years old, America was in the middle of the most deadly war in human history – World War II. I spent my thirteenth year flat on my back with rheumatic fever. My two pastimes during that year were radio and reading. I studied military history, particularly the history of bold military leaders, people who accomplished amazing, audacious things through the people they led. That began a lifelong fascination with the subject of leadership that has carried me through a fifty-five season coaching career.

I have found that virtually all the lessons and principles of leadership that apply to war also apply to football – and to life. The leadership principles that achieve great results on the battlefield also achieve great results in a church, in an office, in a classroom, on a football field or basketball court, or anywhere else a leader seeks to reach a goal through people.

Coaching is leadership. Successful coaching is winning through other people. As a coach, if you don't know how to motivate and inspire other people to win, you lose. My success as a coach, then, is directly proportional to my ability to understand and apply the principles of leadership in everyday situations."

—*Bobby Bowden*

Chapter One:

FOREST AND TREES, GOT IT

"Where do I think Florida State will finish this year? If you can tell me what our injuries will be and what kind of leadership the seniors will provide, I could just about tell you what our final record will be."

—BOBBY BOWDEN

T he process of examining the dimension of vision in terms of leadership with Bobby Bowden has to start with his overwhelming commitment to his faith. Player after player, coach after coach through close to 300 interviews all reflected on that facet of his life.   It was the first quality many of them wanted to discuss.

"I never made football my god," said Bowden.   "I tell people when I speak that you can substitute your job or whatever you perceive as the most important thing in your life where I put football.   But I never made football No. 1.   It was always God first, family second and football third.   You keep it in that order and you'll do okay."

Throughout this book you will read testimony after testimony of how Bobby Bowden's life of faith motivated, inspired, challenged, consoled, reassured and fortified everyone with whom he came in contact.

Wide receiver Peter Warrick was a consensus All-American for Bobby Bowden's 1999 National Championship team, which was the first in the history of the Associated Press poll to go wire-to-wire through a season as the No. 1 ranked team. Warrick scored a Sugar Bowl record 20 points with two touchdown catches, a punt return for a touchdown and a two-point conversion in the Seminoles 46-29 win over Virginia Tech for the BCS title. "Whenever I had problems, I'd go to coach and get great advice," said Warrick. "He was a god-fearing man and he'd say, 'Peter, go to God and pray about this situation or that decision facing you.' Coach did not just talk about his Christian faith, he lived it."

Terry Warren played defensive end for Bobby Bowden and Florida State from 1984-87, as did his brother Scott it the same position from 1976-79. He sums up the legacy of Bowden's faith, for hundreds of others by saying, "When I was playing for coach, I saw a godly man who never wavered in his testimony. That man's life impacted so many young athletes because of his Christian leadership. We'll never know the number. Guys I thought were unreachable for the Lord are now deacons in their churches or in full-time ministry. Coach was planting seeds all the time. He never missed a chance to lead."

Todd Rebol played linebacker at FSU from 1992-95 and talked about his head coach's enduring success. "One way to measure leadership is by the endurance of an individual," he said. "Any leader can have that special season in sports or business where the right set of talent and circumstances come together perfectly. But with Coach Bowden, it was his volume of work. Thirty-five seasons at FSU with all those wins and players and coaches who came out of the program. It shows an endurance factor unique to great leaders.

"There was a stability factor to coach as a leader and staying the course is not always easy. In the music industry there are a lot of one-hit wonders out there. It's the same in coaching. Making it more impressive for Coach Bowden was doing it in college football where you have to do a full reload every four years. That makes it a lot harder."

Daryl Dickey coached quarterbacks for Bowden at Florida State from 2001-07. "Bobby was driven and motivated and was very skilled in his knowledge of the game of football," he said. "But with all of that, he had his life all together. That's a tough thing to do in this profession. Coach Bowden proved it could be done."

George Henshaw coached with Bowden at Florida State and sent his son to play tight end for him from 2002-05. "Coach Bowden has strong convictions on why he is on this earth," he told me. "He believes that God has placed him here for a reason and wants him to live his life the way the Lord wants him to. Coach truly believes that God gave him a gift to relate to young athletes and he is responsible to deliver that gift as long as he is able."

Doug Charley played safety at West Virginia from 1969-73. He said: "There was never any panic around the program, nor was there any blame. We always felt that everything would be alright because Coach had a good plan going at all times. As a result we had confidence in him."

Bowden's openness about his faith has meant everything to current Georgia head coach Mark Richt, who cut his coaching teeth as an assistant at Florida State.

Tragedy struck the Seminole football family in 1986 when popular and outgoing offensive tackle Pablo Lopez was murdered on-campus. A disagreement had turned heated and someone left to get a gun. Lopez was shot standing on the sidewalk and never saw it coming. The team was devastated.

Bowden, of course, took the leadership role during the next few days and spoke at a service on campus. The team was seated in the front of the auditorium which was filled to overflowing with staff, students and faculty.

Bowden drew a deep breath, cleaned his glasses, which was his way of collecting himself, and gave a speech that will never be forgotten by those in attendance.

He talked of the senselessness of the situation and of the value and character of the young man who lay before him. He tried to comfort family and friends who were in attendance and encouraged all to go on living. Then, he leaned forward on the make shift pulpit and let words of emotion spill from his heart.

Bowden challenged all in the room in a way that only he can. Some describe it more as a push than a pull.

"Where is Pablo now?" he asked the tear-filled audience. "Where would you be now? Pablo didn't know he was going to die that night. You don't know if you're going to die tonight. I don't know when I'm going to die. But I do know where I'm going."

That challenge hung heavy in the air. And listening with a growing panic inside was a young graduate assistant coach who had played quarterback for the Miami Hurricanes.

At the end of his message, Bowden looked at the team and invited any one of them to come by his office at any time if they needed to talk to him.

Richt, who was that young coach, met Bowden at his office door the next morning. He admitted he was troubled by the fact that he didn't know the answer to "where he would be" if something happened to him. Bowden led Richt to Christ that very morning.

NO ONE SAID IT WAS EASY

Perhaps there has been no American leader any more historically appreciated and unanimously revered as George Washington. The iconic figure of General Washington astride his beautiful mount leading his new nation in their quest of freedom from Britain is as American as it gets.

History has been appropriately kind to Washington, but it will come as a surprise to many I would guess that he was the subject of wide spread derision and even death threats just a few years after the Revolutionary War.

The colonists who were rapidly growing into their new roles as Americans became infuriated with Washington when it was discovered that he had made a secret treaty with France in an effort to avert a second war with Britain just two years after the Revolutionary War.

Newspaper headlines screamed about Washington's "underhanded deal" and the population of the few cities that existed began to reach near riot status. It was no small political feat for Washington to tamp down the revolt and preserve his place in history.

I wanted to begin with that overlooked piece of history to illustrate that no leader worth his salt ever strolled through a career without extremely difficult challenges. In fact in most cases it is in the overcoming of these challenges that great leaders emerge. The career of Bobby Bowden is no different.

But what do great leaders do when faced with these difficult times? What did George Washington do? More to the point, what did Bobby Bowden do?

Bowden and his family have lived their lives in the public eye for over 60 years and Bobby in particular has faced difficulties that at times drew national attention. The 1974 season at West Virginia was as difficult as it got professionally for Coach Bowden.

Bobby was in his fifth year as head coach of the Mountaineers and a bevy of returning talent and loads of preseason press had hungry West Virginia fans tremendously excited about the season. One former West Virginia player described the fans as ravenous. But the highly anticipated season would prove the low point of Bowden's early career. Long forgotten was the fact that Bowden lost both his first and second team quarterbacks during the season and had to start a freshman, but history can be cruel in that way. West Virginia lost the season-opener at Richmond 29-25 to everyone's shock, yet rebounded the next week at home against SEC member Kentucky, 16-3. A loss at Tulane and win at Indiana had the team staggering at 2-2 and a subsequent four-game losing streak that began with a 31-24 loss against bitter rival Pitt sent Mountaineer fans into a frenzy.

A For Sale sign was planted in the front lawn of the Bowden's Morgantown home. An effigy of Bobby was hung from a tree on the campus and remained there until one of Bowden's own sons had to shinny-up and cut down the noose holding the hanging figure of his father. Some students hung sheets from dorm windows that suggested Bowden find other employment.

Times were bleak.

"We came up the tunnel at halftime during one of the home games and fans were spitting at us and throwing things," said Dr. Rick Vaglienti, a student trainer at West Virginia from 1974-79 and now a practicing physician. "I looked over at Coach and he was just shaking his head as if to say, 'Forgive them for they know not what they do.' We got in the locker room and Coach Bowden spoke to the team and said, 'Put this out of your mind. They don't hate you; it's me they are after.' "

Here Bowden brings an under-achieving football team through their own fans who are booing and spitting. He must stand in front of those players and provide them with something that tells them all is not lost. He's got to lead them past this moment. All great leaders have faced watershed moments like these and most have used the challenge to make them stronger and more effective leaders.

"Coach was pretty clear in his direction following that 1974 season," said Greg Anderson who played strong safety from 1972-76. "He came in the next year and told the team, 'not one person will be bigger than the program this year.' We had a good year and went to the Peach Bowl to play Lou Holtz's N.C. State team."

I CAN SEE CLEARLY NOW

Bobby and Ann Bowden will be the first to tell you that they did not have a grandiose vision that the Seminole football program would one day become the most consistently successful in the history of college football.

"I didn't take the FSU job thinking that I would be there for a long time," admitted Bowden to longtime *Tallahassee Democrat* Sports Editor and friend Bill McGrotha. "I had my eye on that 1981 schedule. We were scheduled to play Nebraska, Ohio State, Notre Dame, Pittsburgh and LSU all on the road and all in succession. I told Ann that we needed to be somewhere else by then."

You may read that and agree that Bowden did not have a specific plan for his success, but the Bowden's did have an even bigger vision. Bobby and Ann declared that they would follow God's plan in their life and go where He led them.

While Bowden admits that the challenge of that '81 schedule was not something he saw as the key to his future in coaching, he did have the vision to see potential in a Florida State program when most did not. You read earlier of the shambles of a program that Bowden inherited in 1976. Having won just four games over the previous three seasons, insiders at FSU saw Bowden as the last hope of having the big-time college program that so many desired.

To his credit, Bowden saw potential when he was an assistant with FSU in the '60s and got a glimpse of the athletes the Seminoles might be able to recruit if they generated some success on the field. That is exactly what happened, although it was a bumpy and challenging road.

Because of his unique organizational skills and attention to detail, which will be thoroughly examined later on, we have a chance to peek into one of the most significant moments early in a great leader's career. Bowden kept every note from every speech, practice, meeting and game while he was at both West Virginia and Florida State. Therefore, he was able to publish the very first speech he gave his Seminole football team in his book *Bound For Glory*. Here is the message delivered to a beaten down team that had become everyone's choice for Homecoming.

> *"Gentlemen, let me explain the importance of why we're all here together,"* Bowden started. He then paused and looked at both sides of the room before continuing. *"First of all, we've got to have a basic understanding of who's in charge around here. There can never be a question of that.*
>
> *"Well, I am the new guy around here. I'm the head coach. And in the past three years your Florida State football team has managed to win only four games and in the meantime lost 29. Y'all have tried it your way, and where did it get you? Nowhere. Now, I think I know how to win. And from now on at Florida State we're gonna do things my way. If you don't like it, then hit the door. Go somewhere else. Because if winning doesn't mean something to you, then we don't need you. From now on it's going to be an honor to wear a garnet jersey and*

represent Florida State University. We're gonna win again at Florida State."

Bowden himself admitted there were snickers in the room when he started off, but other players quickly quieted the rowdies and he says he could feel the attention in the room. He had a lesson to preach and on this most important of days for him it poured out.

> *"Now, I think that we can turn this program around at Florida State. But, gentlemen, it's going to take a big effort by everyone. We're going to have to push ourselves harder than ever before. We're gonna have to make sacrifices – give up individual goals in order to reach a much bigger team goal. But we can do it – WE CAN WIN AT FLORIDA STATE."*

The room was completely quiet now and all eyes were trained on Bowden, who pulled out a sheet of paper and continued, *"Vince Lombardi, the great coach of the Green Bay Packers, once described that glorious feeling that winners have – the kind of feeling that none of you have enjoyed while at Florida State. He said, 'I firmly believe that man's finest hour, his greatest fulfillment to all he holds dear…is that moment when he has worked his heart out in a good cause and lies exhausted on the field-victorious!'*

> *"That will be our goal. That will be the feeling that we all want to achieve – to feel like a winner, to be able to walk around this campus with the satisfaction of knowing that, 'Yes, we can win.' And in order to get that feeling of confidence, and to begin winning football games, then some things around here have got to change.*

"First of all, we've got to develop a winning attitude and that means self-discipline because self-discipline wins football games. And that's our goal at Florida State – to win football games."

Bowden, according to Phil Bynum who assisted in the writing of *Bound For Glory*, was in full control of the room speaking with a confidence that comes from success. He looked every player in the eye as he glared around the room.

"Now in order to build a winning program and develop self-discipline we've got to make some rules around here. And that means making a commitment to ourselves and to each other that we're going to follow those rules."

Bowden went on to give a few general rules to the team and to describe what sacrifice means. He pointed out to them that they represented not only a great school, but their families and friends back home. His final challenge to his team was powerful.

"Listen up, men," he started. *"I want to point out to you that YOU'RE NOT ORDINARY – YOU'RE NOT AVERAGE. YOU ARE SOMETHING SPECIAL – and I don't want you to ever forget that..."* Stirring words from a man setting the tone for what would be a remarkable career with the Seminoles.

We are all leaders and will face times when we must set the tone for the future. Maybe it's at the family dinner table one night, maybe it's in a new position at work, or maybe you are selected for a leadership role in your church or a social club. Maybe you're taking over an entire new branch of the company.

Where did Bobby Bowden get the inspiration for those words? I think something he told me for this book answers that question.

"My dad gave me some good advice," Bowden said. "He said, 'Bobby, don't forget as you go through life, that you're as good as anybody.' "

"You want to know what significance that had on me?" Bobby admitted. "I had a tendency to feel inferior, to feel I couldn't do some of the things I wanted to do. He was trying to tell me I could. And as I went through life, I found it to be true.

"I always wondered where my dad got that advice and I think back to when he came up during the Depression. A lot of people lost so much including their pride and their identity. He never did and I think he thought that was important."

Bowden took a leadership lesson from his father delivered in Birmingham probably 35 years earlier and applied it to his first FSU team.

Nebraska's Tom Osborne would square off against Florida State eight times, with the Seminoles winning six of those games including the 1993 Orange Bowl for the National Championship. The two had tremendous respect for one another. "I was always impressed with the fact that Bobby had a short Bible study every morning with his staff and he continued that practice throughout his coaching career," said Osborne. "This was illustrative of the fact that Bobby always was a man of faith first. He conducted his coaching activities accordingly and I think this gave him the strength and direction to maintain a good perspective on life and the vagaries of coaching. Bobby's sense of humor was another great strength. He was always an enjoyable person to be around."

Mike Shumann was one of the few stars Bowden inherited on his first FSU teams. Shumann, who went on to play in the NFL and earned a place in the FSU Athletic Hall of Fame, sat in that first meeting with Bowden. "When Coach arrived at FSU he had a strong sense of what he wanted to do," he said. "He took over a program in shambles and applied his coaching philosophy at once. We listened because we wanted someone to lead us. We were willing followers."

Florida State finished with a 5-6 record in that first season in 1976 and most of those same players were on the team the following year when the Seminoles jumped to a 10-2 finish. With that sparkling record came a No. 14 Associated Press national ranking and a Tangerine Bowl invitation. FSU backed that season up the next year with an 8-3 record in 1978 and Bowden was making waves in the recruiting wars with a stingy defense and wide-open offensive style that was rapidly gaining the attention of high school players in Florida.

And it was not just FSU fans and players who noticed.

National power LSU was on the hunt for a football coach in 1979 and began to quietly woo Bowden behind the scenes. He was contacted by the Tigers' athletic director several times during the season with coded phone messages left from his "uncle." Bowden admits he was "flattered" by the attention and with that daunting '81 schedule on the horizon, Bobby and Ann began to seriously consider LSU.

It should be made clear now that where most people label events ironic, Bobby Bowden believed that God was leading him throughout his life. So the "irony" that FSU just happened to be playing LSU in Death Valley on October 27, 1979 was not a coincidence in his mind. And Bowden's confession to the media years later serves as a perfect illustration of vision as part of leadership.

"I talked with Ann and decided that if we go over there with a good football team and lose to LSU, then maybe we can't go much further at Florida State and I should take the job," Bowden said. "But if we go over there and win, maybe we can stay right here and get it done."

Florida State did "get it done" in Baton Rouge beating LSU 24-19 and averting a crisis that most Seminole fans never realized was brewing. With the win, Bowden immediately elevated his vision for the program and set his sights on making Florida State a player on the national scene.

"Coach Bowden had the ability to gain the support and the consensus of all the people important to the program – administrators, assistant coaches, players, parents, fans, and donors," said Mike Parsons who was a student sports information staffer at West Virginia with Bowden from 1974-75 and rose to become one of the Mountaineer's top athletic officials. "He just had a magical skill in regard to all of those he was leading. The way Coach did it was his ability and willingness to articulate his message to everyone. He was a great fan of the media and spent time with them. He'd also go out and spend time with fans, alumni and donors which is almost a lost art today."

Bowden used the same skills that Parsons recognized when he came to Florida State. He knew he needed help to make his vision a reality and he shared his vision with the media, players, fans and just about anyone else who would listen.

"Bobby was a great leader because he had a vision of where he wanted to take the team and a plan of how to get there," said longtime friend and frequent opponent Lou Holtz. "He wanted to win and he wasn't afraid to lose, so he and his team were always loose."

Holtz and Bowden were indeed friends and frequent foes on the football field and while different in many respects, their affection for each other was always evident, if surprising, given the results of one of their first meetings, as well as a historic final game.

In 1973 Holtz took an undermanned William & Mary team to West Virginia where they suffered a predictably humiliating loss. Holtz was particularly angry at Bowden as the clock wound down. West Virginia continued to throw the football late in the game and Bowden kept his starters in longer than Holtz felt necessary. "I was not happy because I thought they were running up the score," said Holtz. "When I got to Bobby at the end of the game I told him what I thought and he looked at me and told me, 'Lou, it's not my job to hold down the score – that's your job.' I never forgot that."

While the two figurative giants met a number of times in between, the FSU at Notre Dame game in 1993 was one of the biggest in college football history. The Seminoles were ranked No. 1 and headed to South Bend to play Holtz's second ranked Irish. The media tabbed it the "Game of the Century" and ESPN's young *GameDay* television program thought the event so important that the producers twisted the arms of executives to allow Chris Fowler, Lee Corso and Craig James to go live from the stadium, starting that popular tradition.

Florida State moved through Notre Dame's defense like a hot knife through butter on their first possession scoring on a nearly effortless Charlie Ward to Kevin Knox pass, but it would be the last easy thing for FSU all day.

Notre Dame played hard-nosed, ball-control football and were always one step ahead of the Seminoles. The game still came down to the final drive. Eventual Heisman Trophy winner Charlie Ward led the Seminole offense down the field with cool precision until the Irish defenders dug in their heels in the shadow of their own goal posts. The last play of the game was a Ward pass into the end zone that fell incomplete, ending what appeared to be Bowden's best chance so far at a national championship.

"Coach's first words to us in the locker room were to keep our heads up," said Matt Frier, who was one of the team captains and a senior wide receiver. "We kind of thought we had lost everything and Coach starts talking about how we shouldn't fall that far in the polls and that we had big games against great teams still to go and we could climb up there. By the time he finished talking, a lot of us were thinking about what was coming up instead of having just lost. In hindsight, it was really brilliant."

Bowden, as he so often did, would prove prophetic in that South Bend locker room. Notre Dame inexplicably lost the very next week at Boston College and FSU was right back on its way to its first national title.

Another head coach that Bobby Bowden had a great deal of respect for was Jim Grobe from Wake Forest.

"Bobby was a humble leader," said Grobe. "When you would see him at a meeting you would think 'there's the great Bobby Bowden.' But Bobby never put on airs and tried to act like a big shot. You'd never know Bobby Bowden was Bobby Bowden. If you ever beat his team, which was rate, he was always gracious to you and never blamed his team or coaches. If you lost to him, he would always tell the press what a good team you had and offer high praise.

"At one point, we beat Florida State a couple of times. After one of those games, I met Bobby at midfield and he said, 'Jim, you ought to be ashamed of yourself.' I thought, 'Oh, no! What have I done to offend this legend?' Then he laughed and said, 'Beating an old man like me.'"

"He was a man of principle and character and had his priorities straight for himself, staff and players. He always wanted to set a good example and lived his faith in front of the world and never backed off from his beliefs. There aren't many out there like him."

"What you saw with Coach is what you got," said Florida State All-America defensive tackle Corey Simon. "It didn't matter who was around him or what the circumstances, he was always who he was. Coach knew himself and trusted himself to be who he was. That quality alone made him a great human being. That's leadership."

Ultimately, the measure of vision is whether you can impart that vision on those you lead. Artie Owens played running back for West Virginia from 1972-76 and it is clear that Bowden's message got through to him: "Bobby Bowden taught me three vital lessons in life that gave me stability and an understanding of what I'm doing in life," said Owens. "He taught me that first I needed to have an education and I'm so glad now for all the study halls and the academic discipline. Second, he taught me diligence. I learned that nothing happens unless you stick with it and persevere through the tough times of life. Thirdly, I learned that a faith-based life is the best path to take."

IF YOU'RE SCARED GET OUT NOW

Vision alone will not get one very far. Every coach who has taken over a team has promised the gathered media, alumni, or owners that they can take the team to the top. New executives always have a plan to make their corporation number one and bankers will tell you that their loan officers hear pledge after pledge from potential business owners with the next big thing.

Vision has to be backed up by other qualities like passion and energy.

While Bowden was busy raising the expectations for Florida State football, he was also raising the bar for the players. "Coach had the uncanny ability to take a guy like me, who didn't understand his full capabilities, and then bring it out of you," said one of the Seminoles all time great linebackers, Paul Piurowski, who starred at FSU from 1977-80 and whose game-changing tackle at Nebraska gave FSU what Bowden considers the most important win in school history in 1980. "It was like a chef who takes a whole bunch of rotting bananas and turns it into a delicious dessert. Coach Bowden could see what others didn't, including me. He saw more in you than you did."

Leaders often draw inspiration and frequently find their passion and energy renewed when a challenge arises. The best business leaders dive head first into their work after a disappointing sales quarter, a great mayor stands tallest when his city is facing a crisis, and a leader works hardest when his club is losing members.

Bowden found renewed passion from an unlikely source – his arch-rival.

The University of Miami, under the gregarious leadership of head coach Howard Schnellenberger, won the National Championship in 1983. In addition to being the Seminoles' oldest football rival, Miami was a small private school without the huge alumni base and historic football tradition that most felt essential for college football success.

"There is no doubt that Miami winning it all changed our thinking," said Bowden. "It certainly changed mine. We knew they had a great coach and great athletes to recruit from but back then you weren't supposed to win it all unless you were Alabama or Notre Dame or USC. I think the thing it did for us as a coaching staff is to make us realize that Florida State could get there too. And we better stop worrying about just winning games and go after a national title."

That's leadership at its best. There were no excuses, no "woe is me" mentality, and no jealousy of what their bitter rivals had done. Bowden immediately turned it into a challenge, a motivation, a goal, while ramping up his own personal energy and enthusiasm toward reaching the next step.

"At the beginning of fall practice, you would think that it was his first year of coaching," remembers Sue Hall his longtime administrative assistant. "I never saw him down. He absolutely loved coaching. He loved his players, his coaches and he loved what he was doing."

Georgia head coach Mark Richt worked his way up from graduate assistant coach to offensive coordinator under Bobby Bowden before taking over the Bulldog program in 2000.

"I was always impacted by his passion and his compassion," said Richt. "He had a passion for coaching, competing and watching young men grow. Coach truly cared for all of us he was overseeing. He was my teacher at FSU and I took all of his lessons with me to Georgia. What he was selling, I was buying as a coach and a man."

Florida State linebacker Buster Davis saw the passion as well. "Look, I just about lived in his office my first two years," admitted Davis. "I was going to leave. I had this situation, that situation. But what I remember is the passion that Coach Bowden had for his players and his program. I could feel it when he came to my home to recruit me. Later on I could see that it didn't matter if he was recruiting, talking to booster groups, playing in a golf tournament or going to a banquet. Coach had a passion for Florida State."

If you follow any successful organization, you will find a leader at the top who has that same kind of passion that Bowden's players and coaches saw.

DON'T LEAVE ANYTHING OUT ON THAT FIELD

A leader has a responsibility beyond all others in the organization – he or she has to finish. In football terms, the leader can't just get the offense into the red zone, he's got to get into the end zone.

Among the myriad of staggering records that Bobby Bowden set over his coaching career, one of the most impressive to his peers was his ability to win bowl games.

Bowden's last game at FSU came in the 2010 Gator Bowl against, ironically, West Virginia. He was taking his 28th straight Seminole team to a bowl game which was (and still is at 29 games) the nation's longest consecutive streak. And the second place school is nine bowls behind that. But even more remarkable is that Bowden-coached teams didn't just get to the bowls, they won them. From 1985-1996, Bowden went 14 consecutive years without losing a bowl game. Fourteen! And these weren't the Timbuktu Bowls – they were Sugar Bowls against Auburn and Fiesta Bowls against Nebraska and Orange Bowls against Notre Dame and national championship games against both the Huskers and the Hokies.

Bowden was the ultimate finisher with a 22-10-1 record in bowl games that places him second all-time behind Joe Paterno and just ahead of his hero, Bear Bryant.

"Our staff always did a great job in bowl preparation," Bowden would say after his career was over. "We had a routine that we felt very good about and we stuck to that. It is amazing when you think about it because a bowl game can be very difficult. The other team has plenty of time to game plan for you. Of course you do too, but you have got to manage that long layoff between the Florida game for us and the bowl. You have the distraction of the trip and the city you're playing in. And you have to strike that balance in terms of how hard you work them. They are usually pretty tired of football by then.

"That's one of the reasons that I always liked to play a good team in a big bowl," said Bowden. "I would tell our athletic director to get us in the best bowl he could. I felt like that would keep the boys' minds in the game if they had a big-time opponent."

Bowden didn't lean on overt motivational tools very often and even less on props, but he did dangle one carrot in front of every team.

"I never had an undefeated team up until 1999," said Bowden. "So, I never had a team picture hanging in my office. I used to keep an empty picture frame in there and tell the squads that I wanted to fill that thing with a perfect team one day. After we beat Virginia Tech in the Sugar Bowl to become the first wire-to-wire AP national championship team, our athletic director had a picture frame with him in the locker room. It took us a while, but we finally filled that frame."

Twenty-two bowl trophies and 12 ACC championship rings sit in the FSU trophy cases covering the Bowden era, but the program's biggest lesson in finishing might have come in a tie.

Coming off his first-ever national championship in 1993, Bowden's '94 team had to replace 12 starters, including Heisman Trophy winner Charlie Ward, leading tackler Ken Alexander, three of its top four wide receivers and the entire offensive backfield. FSU never slowed down, however, losing only at Miami (34-20) and boasting a 9-1 record going into the home finale against Florida.

The first three quarters were a disaster for the Seminoles and their streak of consecutive Top 4 finishes appeared to be going down the drain. The Gators were running the Seminoles out of their own stadium and led 31-3 in the fourth quarter. Dumbstruck FSU fans headed for the exits, while Florida supporters started their victory party.

It would have been easy, natural even, for Bowden and his Seminoles to quit. But that was evidently the last thing on their minds.

Quarterback Danny Kanell took charge of the huddle and picked up the pace. Firing passes with pinpoint accuracy and mixing in running plays that suddenly made UF look tired, Florida State started storming back. Fans turned their cars around in the parking lots as FSU cut it to 31-10, then 31-17 and within a blink of an eye it was 31-24. Seminole defenders on the field were screaming at UF's offense to hurry up and snap the ball as they snagged interceptions and sacked the quarterback like they were going through drills. With 1:45 left in the game, Rock Preston ran up the Gator's gut for a touchdown that capped an NCAA record 28-point comeback and tied the game at 31-31.

Florida fans couldn't believe what they had seen, media members couldn't believe what they had seen, Seminole fans who left early couldn't believe that they missed it and FSU players had a 31-31 "win" for the ages.

"I thought about going for two after the last score," an elated Bowden would say. "But I told my team after the game that I just couldn't risk losing that for them. They had worked so hard to get us back to a chance for a tie. I just could not risk them working for all that and then getting a loss. They had to run a few more plays at the end and I thought maybe we could catch 'em one more time," Bowden said with a wink.

It would have been easy in those last few moments for Bowden to say, "You know, there's no way we can win this game. No one has ever come back from 28 points in the fourth quarter. I think we'll just quit." What if Kanell had quit? What if Clifton Abraham had decided to relax instead of getting that first interception? What if the offensive line had decided they were just too tired to beat their heads in when they were that far behind?

When your vision is so clear that it demands you hang in there through the tough stuff and get over the mountains and through the valleys, then your finish will be rewarded. For Bowden and his team, the reward came in winning the national title after that loss to Notre Dame in 1993 and in the 31-31 "win" over Florida.

For you, hanging in there against all odds and finishing strong may result in a turnaround in your company. Or whipping a substance abuse problem. Or repairing a broken marriage. Or finally getting into medical school.

You must not give up on anything because giving up stays with you the rest of your life. Bowden said: "Quitting gets really easy after that first time. You do it once and the next time it's just so much easier to give up and go and try and find something that isn't so hard. Don't start and you won't have to stop."

Who better to wrap up the chapter on vision than Charlie Ward? Winner of the 1993 Heisman Trophy, Ward led Bowden and Florida State to the national championship in 1993. He played 12 years in the NBA and is now a high school coach. He asked his former coach for advice recently and told me, "When I first started coaching at Westbury High (Houston, Texas), I sought advice from Coach Bowden. He shared with me two key points: Be fair with your players and when you make a mistake or error, admit it, apologize and take responsibility. And be honest with the guys. Whenever you make a promise make sure you can deliver. Never get caught telling a lie or fudging the truth."

Now that is good direction for a proper vision!

Chapter Two

DO YOU HEAR ME; IS THIS ON?

"Hiring good people plays a key role. I'm always trying to get balance. I've always been taught if everybody is the same it's not good. You need a mean guy, and you need a nice guy."

—BOBBY BOWDEN

e have established that vision is absolutely critical to effective leadership and we have seen that Bobby Bowden's vision for his programs at all four coaching stops; Howard, South Georgia College, West Virginia and Florida State made him an outstanding leader. However, vision without communication is going to lead to a whole lot of nothing.

A leader who has great plans but can't communicate those plans to his workers is going to experience a great deal of personal frustration. Vision without communication usually ends up leading to nothing more than a dream. In order for your vision to become a reality, you must communicate and sell it so that "your" vision becomes "their" vision.

So the obvious question is how do you communicate a vision? How did Bobby Bowden's vision of West Virginia as a wide-open offense or

Florida State as a powerhouse rather than a doormat become the vision of the players, coaches and even fans of his teams? How did Bobby Bowden convince Sammie Smith, Deion Sanders and Odell Haggins that they would be better off turning down established programs for a chance to build a dynasty at Florida State? How did he make playing for FSU so rewarding that players like Peter Warrick, Warrick Dunn and Corey Simon choose not to go early to the NFL?

SOLD ON THIS ONE

The single most important key to good communication is the belief that it is important to communicate. Proper communication can make the responsibility of leadership so much easier.

Have you ever run across someone in your life, maybe even in the office next to you right now, who asks you a question and halfway through your answer they are asking another question? There is little if any listening going on. Communication, at least on my end, tends to shut down immediately in that situation.

A boss who sits at the conference room desk and asks for input from his employees, but spends his time thumbing through his phone or cuts off the response by engaging another worker is going to create that same communication wall.

One of my favorite illustrations of the power of communication comes from Wal-Mart founder Sam Walton who once said, "Communicate everything you can with your associates (employees) because the more you communicate with them, the more they'll understand and the more they understand the more they'll care, and once they care, there is no stopping them."

This certainly flies in the face of the mentality prevalent in a lot of organizations, even very successful ones, where information is closely contained and on a need-to-know basis. I know the "keep it in the family" communication practice is rampant among coaches today.

"When Coach Bowden talked to you, you bought in and felt you were a very important part of what he was trying to do at FSU," said safety Eric Riley who played from 1981-84. "All of us felt a part of the program's success, star or scout team member. He knew all of our families, our mom's and dad's names. He never forgot that. That made Coach real to us and showed that he really cared."

Bonwell Royal played guard for Bowden at Howard College from 1959-62. He told me, "We admired Coach Bowden and played hard out of respect, not fear. I never heard him swear, but when he said 'dadgummit' we got it in gear. We wanted him to guide and direct us. We liked him because he was effective."

A free safety at West Virginia from 1974-77, Tom Reidemore suggested communication was a gift for Bowden. "Coach had the ability to communicate with people because he spoke on their level," he said. "He understood people and what drives them."

Bobby Bowden believed communication was critical and it started with clear directions.

ARE WE CLEAR HERE?

Rodney Hudson was a two-time All-American offensive guard for the Seminoles and was drafted last year by the Kansas City Chiefs. "Coach was a great communicator," said Hudson. "He knew how to get his point across in a very specific manner. He knew his business because he was a student of football. When he spoke to us, everyone was listening. Coach knew how to interact with players, young and old."

Mickey Andrews was Bowden's defensive coordinator for 25 years and Bowden would be the first to tell you that it is no coincidence that FSU's historic run of Top 4 finishes started when Andrews came on board, "Bobby had a unique way of getting his point across," said Andrews. "During practice, he'd be up in his tower taking notes. The next day he'd ask you to come to his office and say, 'I just noticed something with player so and so. You might want to take a look at him today.' When he said that to you, you would definitely pay close attention to that guy."

"Coach was a clear communicator," said John Hale who played strong safety at West Virginia from 1967-71 and captained the 1970 team. "Coach could take a complete game plan and break it down to its simplest terms. He'd go down the list point by point and show you how to beat that week's opponent."

Byron Capers, a cornerback for FSU from 1993-96, put it this way, "His greatest strength as a leader were his verbal skills. He knew how to engage with each individual and as a result knew what to say, how to say it, and when to say it. Coach would get in our heads so we understood his objectives and purposes. He always knew what motivated us because he was so personal with us."

Sean Muhammed led the Seminoles in rushing in 1993 although he was Sean Jackson at the time. "Coach tried to be very fair with all of us. He had an open door policy and was always available to us when we needed him," he said.

DING, DING, DING

No one is talked "at" more than an athlete. They get lectured to, preached at, implored with and yelled at more than any group shy of maybe boot camp newbies – and that only last six weeks. How many team meetings did Dan Marino sit through? Jerry West? Hank Aaron? Making the routine interesting is a gift that leaders should develop.

"Coach was a great leader who was always colorful and interesting," said FSU consensus All-America offensive guard Jamie Dukes.

"If you're boring as a rock, people will turn you off real quick. By the time I got to the NFL, Coach had taught me how to carry myself and be a man. I knew how to communicate with others which helped as a NFL player and now as an analyst."

Kevin Steele coached linebackers for Florida State in the late 2000's and is now the defensive coordinator at Clemson. He had an appreciation for the way Bowden would deliver a message. "He was just so great at saying things in a way that drove the point home without always pointing the finger," said Steele. "One day we had a star player light it up in a scrimmage. He even hurt two guys. Coach came over to me and said softly, 'Is number 34 going to be any better if he keeps practicing?' I said, 'No sir.' Then Coach said, 'That's what I think.' I got the message very quickly and sat him down the rest of the day.

"I remember another time when we were all gathered at the long coaching table with Coach Bowden at the head. Two assistants started arguing loudly at the other end. Coach didn't slam the table or start yelling. He just said, 'Hey fellas, I thought I was the head coach here – did that change?' End of argument."

West Virginia's Garrett Ford said he still utilizes the communication lessons he learned under Bowden today as he works with young athletes. "Coach could talk calmly and still get his point across clearly," Ford said. "He taught me to look people in the eye when you're talking to them. You always knew where you stood with Coach. He knew how to be firm, but fair and he could put the fear in you when necessary."

Longtime FSU assistant coach Jim Gladden appreciated this quality in Bowden. "You never, ever, walked out of a meeting wondering what the heck he was talking about," said Gladden. "His directions were clear, no ambiguity, and usually during the course of giving you your marching orders he would have gotten you to talk to him about how you were going to get it done. So you would leave a meeting not only with a mission, but a well understood path to achieve the mission. It sure made coaching with him easy."

Apparently, it made it easier on his players as well. "Coach was a great motivator and it came about by the way he talked to us – he told it like it was," said West Virginia's offensive guard from 1972-75, Bob Kaminski. "He didn't beat around the bush."

The Athletic Director at West Virginia during much of Bowden's tenure was Leland Byrd and he told me that Bobby's communication skills extended well beyond his football players. "Bobby was an excellent communicator with his players and staff, and he was just as great with the fans and media," he said. "In fact, he just captivated the media in this state."

An effective communicator can quickly expand both his sphere of influence and his list of accomplishments. FSU's administration recognized quickly that they had captured lightning in a bottle with a personable football coach who could back it up on the field. Soon Bowden found himself not only recruiting the best athletes he could find, but the school started using their head coach to recruit faculty and top scholastic students as well.

"We had a huge win over Florida in 1982 that really showed everybody the importance of a good football team," beloved FSU President Dr. Bernard "Bernie" Sliger told Dr. Jim Jones for his book *FSU One Time!* "We used Bobby to recruit top faculty to come to Tallahassee. We would drop by with top honor students to spend a minute with him. He was pulling the entire university along with his football program."

How many Bowden speeches do you think Dickie Roberts heard in starting 32 straight games at offensive guard for West Virginia? "As a leader, Coach Bowden's communication skills and his sense of humor were superb," said Roberts. "He was always up front with us and never condescending to anyone. After a game when we were watching films, we would get criticized but Coach always did it in a way to get you better."

Chris Potts was a self proclaimed "Yankee" when he played running back for the Mountaineers under Bowden from 1968-71. He said, "Coach had the knack of really using a southern touch which was very effective on some of us. He'd direct you in the way he wanted to go, including the way of the Lord. He recognized that youngsters needed a strong, yet caring leader."

You will read about some of Bobby Bowden's pre-game speeches throughout the book but his practice was to usually give the most inspirational talks the night before the game rather than in the locker room. Naturally, these speeches amounted to communication under the most powerful of microscopes, but no more so than a CEO's address at a critical share holder's meeting, or a pastor at a funeral or a teacher in front of an underachieving class. It seems Bowden rarely missed a home run in these moments.

Current Minnesota Viking and former FSU defensive lineman Letroy Guion said, "His pre-game speeches were great. By the time he was done, everyone would be fidgeting so badly and you couldn't wait to get out there."

"Coach had an incredible way of speaking to his players," said former West Virginia defensive lineman Clay Singletary. "It was almost a preacher like quality. When he spoke, you listened. Coach would speak to us at the Friday night dinners before the game. We would be so fired up we'd want to play the game that night. Then I'd think, 'How will he top this next Friday night?' And he always did! His ability to communicate made every player feel part of the team."

Players also agree on the fact that Bowden's voice itself was memorable and that can be important. One wonders if Donald Trump would be as popular on television if his thickly accented *"You're Fired"* weren't so memorable. John F. Kennedy's proclamation of *"Ask not what your country can do for you..."* wouldn't be the same without that New England accent.

"Coach's voice was unmistakable," said former FSU defensive back Bill Ragans. "It was a unique voice and I can still hear him today saying 'hey buddy' or 'now men!'"

Martin Mayhew played cornerback for FSU then six years in the NFL. He is now the general manager of the Detroit Lions and he too hears Bowden's voice. "Yes, I hear his voice today." said Martin. "He's saying 'dadgum it, do it right.' That was his way of striving for excellence at FSU. 'Don't get careless and sloppy out there. I don't want any corner cutting.' I'm not sure Coach gets as much credit as he deserves in terms of handling details."

Zack Crockett was FSU's fullback in 1992-94 and played 12 seasons in the NFL. He said, "I can still hear his voice today – 'C'mon now boy. C'mon Zack. Get after him.' The man was always genuine and he taught us to be the same. All that was important to carry over to the rest of your life."

Coach Bowden's ability to clearly and concisely communicate allowed him to hold his players and coaches accountable because there was no doubt where the responsibility lay.

Dan Footman played defensive tackle at FSU and his son Dan Hicks is a sophomore on the 2011 FSU team. "Coach always told us to be responsible for our actions and to never embarrass yourself or the program," said Footman. "As an athlete, it's so easy to get in trouble and end up in the headlines. The best thing I learned was to do what he tells you, 'Stay away from the wrong places and the wrong people.' Whenever we had a problem with the team, Coach would call a team meeting and share his disappointment. Then he'd stress that we had to be accountable for our actions. There was never too much doubt."

"Coach really believed in accountability," said FSU alum Connell Spain. "With his players, he'd give you a second chance but he held your feet to the fire. He wanted us to be men, but to do that your character needed to be untarnished. It would become your DNA."

Six year NFL cornerback and a star safety for the Seminoles in the late '80s, Dedrick Dodge made it seem pretty simple. "For coaches and players both, when Coach Bowden opened his mouth everybody listened."

REALLY, ITS JUST A SCRATCH

My passion for the study of leadership and the qualities and traits shared by the most successful leaders has drawn me to a stark realization. One cannot be a successful leader without being optimistic.

To have people follow you, a leader must give them hope for the future. The leader must exude an optimistic vision. Show me a great leader who ever inspired anyone with a barrage of pessimism. "B Company, try and take that enemy tank," or "Offense, I think the sweep might work." See what I mean? But you don't have to take my word for it. President Ronald Reagan said, "Optimism is a choice and one of the most powerful ones you can make." Colin Powell said, "Perpetual optimism is a force multiplier."

My dear friend and one of the founders of the Orlando Magic is Jimmy Hewitt. He is also one of Florida State's staunchest supporters and a longtime friend of Bobby Bowden. Jimmy is a great judge of character and one of the most perceptive people I know. "Bobby was loved and respected by everyone – players, parents, fans and media and the reason was he was always positive and upbeat," he told me. "There were no negatives with the man. Bobby was admired by everyone because of his love for the Lord, his family and all the people who knew him. As a result, he created unity and chemistry at FSU that was second to none. That sums up Bobby Bowden as a leader for the 35 years I was with him."

John Davis brought the lumber from his safety position at FSU from 1989-92 and he remembers Bowden's up-beat nature. "He was a man who talked the talk and walked the walk," said Davis. "He didn't have to talk about his Christian faith because he radiated it. The man just glowed as a result. Coach was always positive no matter the situation. He was a glass half-full guy at the very worst. That optimism rubbed off on his players and coaches."

"Coach Bowden would come up to me at practice out of the blue and just talk a little bit," said FSU's 11th all-time leading scorer, kicker Bill Capece. "He would ask us how we were doing and tell me he was proud of me. That gave me such a special feeling and encouraged me through the daily grind of practice."

We hear again from Bowden's assistant Sue Hall. "Coach would never berate a player or coach in front of the group," she said. "He would always pull them aside in his office if he had something to discuss. It was part of his personality to keep things positive and keep spirits high."

"Coach had wonderful people skills and had a great way of putting others at ease," said Jimbo Fisher who became FSU's first new head football coach in 34 years when Bowden stepped down. "When you went to him with a problem, you came away expecting everything to be okay. Coach had an optimistic outlook on life and it rubbed off on all of us."

Bowden turned to highly respected offensive line coach Rick Trickett to resurrect the program in 2007, hiring him from West

Virginia. "Coach saw the best in everybody," said Trickett. "He had his way of saying things to you so you'd get the point."

Seminole linebacker Willie Pauldo's observations showed Bowden's ability to instill hope. "You felt good and secure when he spoke to you even when it wasn't about football," said Pauldo. "His main mission was to help his football players grow up and be successful and mature men. He did very well at that."

Would that message of hope serve leaders in homes, churches, schools and businesses well today? You bet it would. Our nation needs a message of hope right now. Our leaders need to inspire hope. Remember the quote we referenced earlier, "There is nothing to fear, but fear itself"? It is essentially a plea for hope.

DID WE JUST DO THAT?

The ability to motivate and inspire people is just part of a leader's job description. My study of leadership leads me to a firm belief that you must be a student of how to motivate. You can learn to be a better motivator. The key is the study of your people and what their motives are in life.

Each person needs to be dealt with in a different way, but we all need inspiration and motivation on a daily basis. Inspiration comes from the outside; the ultimate goal is to have people self-motivated on the inside. It must be on our mind every day.

Bowden was a master motivator.

Skip Holtz is the highly successful head coach of the University of South Florida and he led the University of Connecticut to national prominence before that. He knows just a little bit about motivation since he is the son of "Mr. Motivation" Lou Holtz. Skip's first football coaching job was a graduate assistant under Bowden.

"You would walk away from a meeting with him and think, 'If there's a nicer guy on the planet, I'd like to meet him,'" said Holtz. "He just made you feel so good about yourself. He didn't motivate through fear and intimidation. He'd do it in such a way that you wanted to run through a wall for the guy. Just a great people person."

West Virginia's head manager from 1972-76 was Bob Pitrolo. "I never heard Coach use a cutting personal comment to chastise a player," he said. "He'd get after a player for his actions, but it would never be about him as a person. His comments to a player were always designed to get more effort from him. Coach didn't get the best talent at West Virginia, but he'd make underachievers become overachievers by treating them that way."

Greg Carr was tied for second for career touchdown receptions at Florida State with 29 from 2005-2008. He said, "I remember during one game Coach came to me on the sideline and said, 'You gotta go up and make a play for me NOW.' He had me so ready to go I thought the ball would never come down. I just kept telling myself I've got to make this play."

Monk Bonasorte is in FSU's Athletics Hall of Fame for his 15 career interceptions. "Bobby Bowden listened to his players and he'd give each one of us an opportunity," he said. "If you earned it you would play. Coach motivated in such a way that you wanted to be a part of his program. He inspired you to work as a team. All of us wanted to play for him."

"Coach was able to get men to come together and believe in exactly what he was saying and never doubt it wouldn't work," said FSU fullback Lamar Glenn. "One day during bowl practice my junior year, I was walking out to the field when Coach Bowden pulled alongside me in his golf cart. He asked me to sit next to him and said, 'Young man, I've been watching you and the progress you're making.

You are going to get drafted next year.' Well, I didn't think anyone was watching me at practice much less him, but the next year I started every game and was drafted. Coach made you believe in yourself."

Dave Hudson was a backup center at West Virginia from 1968-72. "I went to West Virginia to play football, but it never really worked out," he said. "I had serious knee problems and never could build a career. Through all of that, Coach Bowden treated me with respect and acted as if I was one of the stars. We had our last senior squad meeting and in front of the whole team he said, 'If there's anything I can ever do to help one guy in this room, it is Dave Hudson.' That blew me away. He helped me get into graduate school and that led to a 35-year career with Console Energy Company."

Clint Purvis is Florida State's team chaplain and the person to whom Bowden entrusted the spiritual health of his players. The two are extremely close and continue to spend a lot of time together. "Coach was a great motivator," said Rev. Purvis. "He motivated people by knowing your personality and what makes you tick. He knows you, not about you. He remembers everything about you and your family as well. He knows your strengths, your weaknesses and what makes you laugh and cry. It was not a business to Coach Bowden, it was a ministry. That's why he coached so long and wanted to keep going longer."

"He had really hard practices, but he inspired you to go all out," said Peter McConnell a receiver at West Virginia from 1975-79. "His pep talks were fantastic. He had a gift for words. Coach just had the ability to get 'it' out of you."

Matt Frier was a wide receiver on the Seminoles 1993 National Championship team and one of FSU's most popular players. He talked about how he was sometimes asked whether Bowden was really in charge of the team. "I'd laugh at people who would ask me that and say, 'He has so much control over the team you wouldn't believe it,'" he said. "One day Coach said me, 'Matt, if I get onto you for dropping a pass, I may forget to pump you back up and motivate you. There are over 100 of you players out here and I can't possibly remember everything I say during practice. I might say something that'll keep you up all night. I have ten assistants on the field, so I can chew on them during practice and then pump them up at the end of the day. I can't do that with 100 players. I have to coach the coaches and build them back up. You can't send a broken spirit onto the playing field.' I run a fairly large business now and I follow that Bowden principle every day."

Ray Willis is now playing offensive guard for the Miami Dolphins. He points out that Bowden's motivation had an honest ring to it. "Coach was always pushing you out on the practice field," said Willis. "There was never any doubt that you were out there to work and get better. The depth chart didn't matter to him. He would put his best players out there and let them compete against each other. He wanted the best players to emerge and it was all out in the open."

Let's pause for a second and reflect on that last statement. Wouldn't the most effective general be the one determined to get his very best leaders in charge of every unit? Perhaps every school principal should set up their teaching staff by putting the right people in the right classrooms, no matter their experience level.

Jamal Reynolds won the Lombardi Award in 2000 as the nation's best lineman/linebacker. "I appreciated Coach's approach to motivation," said the former tenth pick of the NFL draft. "He inspired his players which gave us the confidence to go out there and be outstanding. He never cursed us or downgraded us. His mission was to pick us up and give us a lift so we'd play at our best."

The men who coached with Bobby Bowden from the '60s until he retired agreed on his great ability to inspire people.

"Bobby was not a rah-rah type leader," said Wally Burnham who coached linebackers at FSU and is now defensive coordinator at Iowa State. "In our staff meetings, he would sometimes read to us from a World War II book that he had studied thoroughly. He would always point out the hard times and struggles those people had gone through. He did it to inspire us and our reaction would be, 'Let's strive to lead like that. We can do it!' He made us rise to another level with that motivational approach."

Jack Stanton coached with Bowden at FSU in the early years. "Coach was just outstanding at getting his assistant coaches on the same page," he said. "If you were doing your job properly, he let you do it. If Coach respected your abilities, he'd just give you the freedom to work. This motivated me because his fingers were not in your hair all the time."

"Coach had a great feel for people – all of them," said Rick Trickett. "He knew what your strengths and weaknesses were and how to get the best out of everyone. He once told us, 'I lead with a baton and not a whip.' "

Former FSU lineman John Donaldson is now head coach at Marianna High School in Florida and his thoughts also suggest that Bobby Bowden's ability to manage his coaching staff was transparent to the players. "Coach was able to energize his staff," he said. "The assistants were thrilled to be coaching with him and sure didn't want Coach to come down on them. He would get on the coaches to get things corrected and it would then come on down to us on the playing field. Within 24 hours the problems would be corrected."

"Coach inspired us and made us believe we could win every game," said former West Virginia defensive end Andy Reters.

"He inspired you to strive for greatness for yourself and him," said John Harcharic, a safety at West Virginia from 1970-74. "You didn't want to let him down because you knew he cared about you."

Three more former players help sum up the impact of Bowden in terms of motivation and inspiration. "Coach could see into the hearts and heads of each individual so he could motivate them to reach higher, but he always did it in a manner that would benefit the team," said Billy Allen, one of the Seminole's all-time great kickoff return men. "Coach Bowden would give each one of us an opportunity and if you earned it you would play," said FSU Hall of Famer Monk Bonasorte. "He motivated in such a way that you wanted to be a part of his program. He inspired you to work as a team. All of us wanted to play for him." And Gary Lombard, a defensive end at West Virginia from 1972-75, said it succinctly, "Coach conveyed to us the belief that we could do more than most of us thought possible."

One of the payoffs for 34 years of motivation and inspiration at Florida State came before his last game, according to longtime friend and state trooper escort Major Billy Smith. "At the end of the day, Coach Bowden was just an exceptional person and a great leader," said Smith. "When we arrived at the Gator Bowl for his last game it was rainy and kind of miserable. But there stood a tunnel of over 300 of his former players when we pulled up to see him walk into the stadium. It was just overwhelming to feel the love and respect they had for him as he made that walk."

PLEASE ENJOY YOUR DESSERT WHILE WE BRING UP...

I strongly emphasize, as I go around the country, that leadership generally gravitates to the man or woman who can talk. That's generally who we elect to our political office; that's who we hire as our CEO's and it is who we want as our head coaches.

We as followers gravitate towards the leaders who can stand in front of a group, command attention, and effectively communicate. It really is that simple.

The best public speakers do it by telling stories. They realize people are hard-wired to retain stories, not PowerPoint presentations.

Bobby Bowden was a master at this art.

Two stories exemplify Bowden's ability to connect and engage, and they occur on the very biggest of stages.

My co-writer, Rob Wilson, joined Bowden on a trip to Las Vegas for the ESPY Awards in 2000. It was the biggest event that ESPN had ever put on and included just about every major sports and entertainment figure in the country. Michael Jordan was to win the ESPY of the decade (1990-2000) but they were all there: Wayne Gretzky, Andre Aggasi, Peyton Manning, Lance Armstrong, the US Women's Soccer Gold medal team, Mark McGwire, Tiger Woods and on and on. The room across the hall contained an equal flood of celebrities ranging from Tyra Banks to Burt Reynolds.

The event was shown live and treated like the Academy Awards, complete with black tie and seat holders who scrambled into vacant chairs when presenters were ushered back stage.

As we say in the South, it was tall cotton!

Wilson said he started to get a little curious as the night wore on about what Bowden would say in front of this group when accepting the award. He admitted to looking over at Bowden's note pad which he scribbled on throughout the evening. He saw several slashed through ideas.

FSU's award as team of the decade came late in the program and you could tell some of the well-heeled pros were starting to chomp at the bit to get to the casino.

Reynolds, a former FSU running back and dear friend of Bowden's, made the presentation and the room was Bowden's for a few moments.

Bowden grasped the podium and, in the most engaging dialogue you've ever heard, took the audience on a short ride. The story simply isn't that funny in print. If I write it here you'd go "okay." But the punch line refers to him forgetting Ann at home in all the excitement and the punch line was, "Hey, you can't remember everything."

It brought the house down. You can watch the tape of these celebrities just guffawing and Michael Jordan in the front row actually slapping his knee as he cracks up.

Wilson said after the show was over, he was cutting through a back hallway when he saw ESPN personality Chris Fowler was walking over shaking his head. "Every celebrity in the world was in that room and who steals the show, Bobby Bowden," said Fowler.

The second example of Bowden's remarkable public speaking gifts occurred during the Seminoles trip to The White House to be honored as the 1999 College Football National Champions.

The mood during the tour was a little unsettled as the White House staff clearly was still distracted by the Monica Lewinsky affair. If the staff wasn't distracted before the team arrived, they certainly were once they were there, as many whispered questions to the attending staff about what they knew and when they knew it. The questions clearly weren't unique to the FSU tour group.

President Clinton met alone with the Seminole football team without any staff, assistant coaches or White House aides who were all shuffled down to the East Room for the formal presentation. Coach Bowden spent private time with President Clinton in the Oval Office as the team was arranged in front of the group and key members of Senate and Congress began to fill the perimeters of the room.

All eyes turned to the hallway as Hail to the Chief was played and President Clinton and Bowden strolled in like two old friends and moved to the podium. After some preliminary remarks, the President paused and suggested that he thought Bobby Bowden got a bigger round of applause than he did when they were announced.

Bowden stepped in and dead-panned, "Well, I had a better year than you did."

The room was up for grabs and no one was laughing harder than the President. He took some time to collect himself and even had to wipe away tears of laughter before he could go on.

Duke Coach David Cutcliff said, "Coach Bowden had a wonderful ability to communicate. Storytelling was one of his major strengths. He was able to keep young and old alike on the edge of their seats listening to his stories. He was one of the best ever in that department."

Travis Johnson was one of the nation's most highly recruited defensive linemen coming out of high school and traveled all the way from Colorado to play for Bowden in Tallahassee. Now a member of the NFL's Houston Texans, Johnson has similar memories of his coach. "We loved it when Coach would talk to us before practice," he said. "We'd be under the shade trees and he'd start telling us stories. They were always funny. That's when the 'Bowdenisms' would start rolling out of his mouth."

As Bowden's success at FSU grew so did his salary. In fact, he was one of the first college coaches in the country to crack the million dollars a year salary bracket. And once his "pay," as he called it, became fairly well known he had a new line he would use at banquets, churches and award ceremonies. "I'm sorry my wife Ann couldn't make it with me tonight," he would say. "We have always enjoyed (Montgomery, Miami, Michigan, you name it). She certainly would have been here, but she had a previous commitment. She's being inducted into the Master Card Hall of Fame tonight."

We will let our favorite State Trooper sum up the chapter.

"Football was not a life and death issue to Coach," said Billy Smith. "He did his best and was proud of his accomplishments, but his great strength as a leader was that he cared about people. He didn't try to force his opinions or beliefs on others, but he would thoroughly explain what might happen if you decided to do this or that. He'd explain the pluses and minuses and then help lay out a plan for you. Then he'd offer his guidance to help make that plan a reality."

I contend that this is the essence of communication in leadership.

Chapter Three:

PEOPLE WILL REMEMBER A SMILE

"We were at my Grandmother's house with all the family and the FSU coaches. Coach Bowden was talking and my little sister – Latoya – who was four or five at the time, crawled over and put her head in his lap and went to sleep. That was the deal sealer for me coming to Florida State."

—DERRICK BROOKS

To some, qualities like compassion, a sense of humor, the ability to delegate and even learning itself are signs of a weak leader. Nothing could be further from the truth and I can reinforce that having delved into the lives and careers of hundreds of great and diverse leaders. My most recent book on Bear Bryant illustrated it. To many, his gruff voice and legendary preseason football practices captured the essence of a detached dictator. No way! I was flooded with quote after quote that showed "The Bear" could be a cub.

The irony of "people skills" in the modern coaching profession is striking. In a profession filled with machismo, ego and a refusal to compromise, the ability to relate to people just blows by people at times. But it does not blow by the great ones.

I literally had legal pads filled top to bottom, page after page with quotes from players, coaches and staff about the fact that Bobby Bowden's people skills were one of his overwhelming strengths. Bowden appears to be perhaps the most comfortable leader I have studied in terms of allowing his strong people skills to be one of his most visible traits.

Is the most effective corporate CEO the one who relishes barking at subordinates during every staff meeting? Is the most successful general one who recklessly risks his troops to reach the next objective? Are the best parents the ones hanging on the Little League fence demanding to know why their kid wasn't in the starting lineup?

Bobby Bowden's ability to maintain the respect and loyalty of his players, staff and coaches over so many years is linked tightly to his remarkable people skills.

Art Baker, who served as head coach of The Citadel and East Carolina University, was part of a wonderful demonstration of Bowden's skills when he served a season as the Seminole's offensive coordinator in 1986.

Baker was in the press box calling the offensive plays during a game. Bowden, who was famous for getting an itch to call a play or two from the seat of his pants, got on the headsets early in the game and asked Baker, "Art, look at the tight end. I think he could be wide open. Let's try and get one to him."

It is important to note that Florida State coaches had talked in both staff meetings and practice about their opponent's ability to cover the tight end at the last minute with a linebacker. It was a tricky defense that almost baited quarterbacks to throw there.

"Coach, let me take a look at it," said Baker who hoped his boss wouldn't ask again.

But the headsets chirped up a few plays later with Bowden pulling on Baker's sleeve again. "Art, I believe we can rip 'em good with that pass to the tight end."

"Coach," said a hesitant Baker. "We can call it, but I think that linebacker is going to drop right in there."

"I feel good about it; let's call it," came Bowden's directive.

Florida State snapped the ball and the quarterback dropped back, looked up and released a perfect spiral to the tight end who watched as a linebacker stepped in front of it and picked it off.

There was dead silence on the headphones.

It seemed like an eternity until Bowden's voice cracked over the radios. "Art?" asked Bowden.

"Yes sir."

"I see what you mean," was Bowden's reply.

That's how a leader handles a sticky situation. He could have ranted and raved about the interception, but instead he told everyone on his staff, without saying it directly, that he made a mistake, should have trusted his staff, has confidence in everyone and he'll get back to the original game plan.

Bowden's strength in this area was not something he just developed while his Seminole teams were floating among the Top Five teams in the country for 14 consecutive years. He showed these skills early in his career which had a lot to do with where he eventually ended up.

"As an 18, 19-year old kid, Coach made you feel comfortable around him and that's hard to do," said Fran Gleason who played linebacker at West Virginia from 1974-78. "So many coaches rule by fear and intimidation. We knew he was the boss and steering the ship, but he was comfortable to be with."

ASK HIM YOURSELF HE'S SITTING RIGHT THERE

I am told that Email is too slow and impersonal now. You've got to be tweeting and on Facebook. Email is too slow? Why not pick up the phone or walk up two floors and have a personal conversation?

Life moves quickly these days and communication is easier than it has been in the past, but it also can isolate leaders. Today, many leaders climb up into their ivory tower and email or tweet or whatever across the whole of their empire.

There is a ceiling on how great a leader can become if they do not have personal relationships with their workers, or in the case of Bowden and the Bear, his coaches, players and fans.

Bowden observed practices from his tower, but he never led from there. While he was clearly in charge, he never separated himself from his staff and players to the point that there was not a relationship.

History is full of examples of rulers who grew so drunk with power that eventually they had walled themselves off in their castle throne rooms never to be exposed to the subjects they ruled. They ended up breathing their own smoke and believing all of their own stories.

Don Yeager, former *Sports Illustrated* writer and author of the biography of Warrick Dunn called *Running For My Life,* was always struck by Bowden's accessibility and availability. "He was always so approachable and didn't have that CEO mentality," said Yeager. "Players felt they could come to him with any issue and that gave Bobby a unique connection with them. That's a relationship style that is hard to duplicate.

"Coach loved to relate to the players' mothers. If he could get to the mom, he'd generally win the recruiting battle. He really did care about those women and they knew it. He had an inside track to their hearts. That's rare in the sports world."

Sam Cowart, a consensus All-American linebacker for the Seminoles in 1996 and seven-year NFL star, told about when he was being recruited by FSU during his recent induction into the FSU Hall of Fame. "I was being recruited by a lot of big schools," admitted Cowart. "One day at my high school practice there were a bunch of head coaches. Spurrier from Florida was there and about four or five other head coaches. Brad Scott was the offensive coordinator at FSU and he was there, but Coach Bowden wasn't. As I was coming off the field one of the head coaches asked me, 'Where's Coach Bowden?' and kinda laughed. I told them all that he was at my Mom's office all afternoon signing autographs. They all just stopped in their tracks."

"I was just a lowly student manager and Coach Bowden's door was always open to me," said Bob Pitrolo who worked at West Virginia from 1972-76. "I didn't go in that much but any time I needed to talk with him he'd give me the time."

The expression "open door" is really overused today. In fact, there probably has not been a head coach in any sport at any level who has not reassured parents with that "my door is always open" phrase. How many executives take new jobs with the same promise from the boss? How many at the very top really do make themselves accessible? Clearly, Bowden felt it was important.

"Coach's door has been open to me for nearly 25 years," said former Florida State safety John Davis who gained fame for his stadium rocking tackles. "I can call him to this day and he'll be there to talk with me. He is the ultimate human being."

John Flath played offensive line for the Seminoles from 1990-92 and echoes Davis' observations. He says, "Coach Bowden always said you win with people and it wasn't just talk to him. We could go see him about our struggles or seek his advice about whatever we felt was important. That availability is not true of every major college coach out there."

The availability and approachability that Bowden practiced did not emerge when the word "legend" began to be associated with his name. It was in his roots.

Dickie Roberts started 32 games for the Mountaineers at offensive guard from 1967-70. He said, "Coach Bowden never forgot where he came from and as a result, his door was always open to us. We could go talk with him about anything and it was not just football. We could discuss world issues, family struggles, or what to do about our school work. He was always interested and available."

Jerry Johnson was a defensive tackle for the Seminoles in the later 1990s and went on to play for the Denver Broncos. "Coach was a father figure away from home for his players. I always felt comfortable walking into his office, because I could talk to him about anything," he said.

Part of the reason that Bowden had such success with his open door is that he knew how to communicate. He knew that often time people really just want their superiors to hear them. Bowden was a master at getting his point across without judging.

"My strongest memory of Bobby Bowden is how he made me feel as a young man," said W.B. Newton, a West Virginia linebacker from 1970-74. "I struggled with injuries which really rocked my world, so I felt that I'd lost a dream and a purpose. Coach didn't let that affect our relationship. I could stop by to see him at any time. He always made me feel like a human being and not a piece of property. That meant so much to me."

Future Florida State Hall of Fame member Monk Bonasorte was a tough-as-nails safety out of Pittsburgh who played on two of Bowden's greatest defenses in 1979 and 1980. He said, "Bobby Bowden made you feel important when he talked to you. He'd close that office door and let you talk about anything that was on your mind. It could be any topic, but he'd never force his beliefs on you. He would ask you questions that let you get around to the right decision."

Former Seminole offensive lineman John Donaldson made this observation about his head coach. "Coach was always receptive and would listen to you. You may not get what you wanted, but you'd have your say at least," he said.

Paul McGowan was a prototype middle linebacker for the Seminoles in the 1980s. He was named the nation's top linebacker as a senior in 1987 when he took home the Butkus Award. But he learned after his FSU career was over that the relationship Bowden had with his players was anything but typical.

"We could go in and discuss any problems, football or anything else with Coach," McGowan said. "You might talk about school issues, personal problems, or anything else. I played in several all-star games my senior year and spent time talking with other players. I soon discovered that they didn't have the kind of relationship with their head coach that we enjoyed with Coach Bowden. I loved to be around the man."

How powerful would the leaders in our day-to-day world be if they left those kinds of impressions on the people they lead? How effective is a mother or father whose child believes they can ask them anything? How powerful would a pastor be whose congregation felt they were not going to be judged in his office? How successful would a CEO be who bothered to find out how the employees really felt?

Bowden's ear was bent by more than just former players.

"Of all the sports leaders I covered over 45 years in journalism, no one was as approachable and cooperative as Bobby Bowden," said renowned former *St. Petersburg Times* columnist Hubert Mizell. "The explosion of the media in the last 20 years or so has made that tougher and tougher to do. Bobby was the last of that generation of big-time college football coaches who would welcome you into their lives and be approachable at all times – good or bad."

The *Orlando Sentinel's* Brian Schmitz nearly shook his head when speaking of Bowden's openness. He said, "I remember that at least one spring football game, Bowden came up to the press box late in the fourth quarter to talk to the writers because he knew we were on tight deadlines.

"Another time, I needed to ask him a question and tracked him down at a golf course. I waited in the clubhouse as he made the turn. He told me what I needed for my story and then played the back nine. Can you imagine a big-time college coach doing that today?"

My co-writer went one better on Schmitz in terms of the media.

Rob Wilson tells me that the Seminoles were playing a night game in the late 1980s and just drilling the opponent. For years Florida State suffered in newspaper coverage on Sunday mornings because they chose to play their games at night and technology at the time meant deadlines that often fell before FSU games were over.

Florida State was hammering away at the other team when sports information director Wayne Hogan had an idea. He called down to Wilson who was on the sideline and asked him to approach Bowden for quotes that he could give the media.

Wilson said Bowden looked at him like he was crazy and then agreed as long as the opposing coach never found out about it. Hogan gathered the media in the press box and swore them to secrecy. He then typed out quotes that Bowden relayed to Wilson while standing at the edge of the bench.

DID I HEAR THAT JUST RIGHT?

Experts will tell you that listening is quickly becoming a lost art. Is *Tweeting* more about listening or pushing out the sender's opinion? Is *Facebook* more about me or you? Are people reading more or less than they have in the past?

The best leaders listen. The most successful leaders are hungry for information. Bobby Bowden was good at listening. In fact, the last real planning he did before any game was all about listening.

Mickey Holden, who filmed a documentary surrounding an entire season for ESPN, talks about the "what if" sessions as a clear example of Bowden's skills in organization and preparation, but the practice was also a strong lesson in the value of listening.

Bowden instituted the "what if" sessions while at Florida State as a last check on the entire plan for his Seminoles the night before a game. Home or away, Bowden would either meet in his hotel room or his office overlooking Doak Campbell Stadium and put his coordinators and other staff through an exam of sorts.

Bowden would fire questions at his coaches about the game and all the scenarios that could play out. He might ask, "What do you plan to do if we figure out that we can't block that defensive end? What are we gonna start calling if we are down by 21 in the second half. What is your strategy if we can't get the ball away from their offense? What if our kicker can't hit the broad side of the barn? What if the quarterback gets hurt? What if so and so gets hurt?"

"It was not exactly like you were getting grilled, but it also wasn't the most fun you've ever had," said former FSU offensive coordinator and current Georgia head coach Mark Richt. "It was a great way to make sure you were on the same page though. It caused you to think about some things you might not have otherwise and it helped the game calling go smoother the next day. There were times we would be discussing a decision on the headsets and someone would chime in and say, "We talked about this in 'what if' and decided x, y or z."

ESPN producer Mickey Holden spent the entire 2004 season filming a documentary on the season and he remembers the "what if" sessions vividly.

"Coach Bowden allowed total access for the whole season," said Holden, who has produced a number of award winning programs. "The highlight had to be the FSU at Miami game. I rode into the stadium on the team bus and have never heard such cussing and verbal taunts at a college game. The stadium was electric.

"The night before, our cameras had access to the FSU coaches 'what if' meeting. They went over every scenario that might come up and tried to figure out in advance how they'd react. The game unfolded just as expected, except FSU lost on a field goal attempt that went wide left. It was a shocking loss for all these players and coaches.

"I never will forget Bobby Bowden in the locker room with his players after that game. He said, 'We gave it our best. Keep your heads up. We'll learn from this. Failure is temporary. So get ready to play next week.' I will never forget that scene. Coach Bowden had to be crushed and disappointed. However, he demonstrated a sense of calmness, peace and poise. That sticks with me to this day."

The value of this one practice would make the very best leaders even better. A store manager would be better prepared on Black Friday if he sat down the night before with his key managers and worked through the scenarios. Maybe the opening of a business goes smoother because they worked through some nightmare scenarios the night before and were able to adjust. A potential disaster on a new product roll out may be averted because the employee down the line with no direct responsibility with the event makes a casual observation. However, none of this would get anywhere if the person at the top will not listen.

West Virginia tight end Randy Flinchum played from 1967-70 and he saw Bowden change in this respect. He said, "When coach first started out he had some of that boot camp mentality. You know, 'My way or the highway.' But he listened to us and was willing to adapt to some of our opinions."

"Coach was great at empowering other people, which broadened his influence and allowed those coaches to share in the responsibility of the FSU program," said Brett Williams who was an All-America offensive tackle for the Seminoles in 2002. "I think it's a key reason why he maintained his energy and coached as long as he did."

"I was just a kid from Baltimore," said Mark Durham who was a walk-on offensive guard from 1973-78. "I was at a reunion long after I left WVU. Coach was there and didn't remember my name. He did say to me, 'You were a forestry major weren't you?' I said, 'How did you remember that?' Coach replied, 'In all my years of coaching, you were the only forestry major I ever had.'"

Award winning *Orlando Sentinel* columnist Larry Guest was close to Bowden. He told me, "Bobby was a coach who actually listened to people. I think the reason he was such a good listener was that he was a down to earth guy who didn't try to big-time you. Bobby was not into himself like so many high level coaches who carry on a conversation with you as if they were talking to a mirror.

"I didn't always agree with Bobby when I was covering him, but he had the strength to give you your due."

One of the first players Bowden visited when he got the head coaching job at a then floundering Florida State program was Tallahassean Sam Childers, who would be a star at tight end. "Coach made me a good listener," he said. "I've learned to listen to everyone and work with them from my FSU experience. Take in what they're saying because you never know when a good idea may surface."

Dr. Rick Vaglienti was a student trainer for West Virginia from 1974-79 and he and the other young trainers were having a late night snack at Penn State in 1974 – a disastrous season for Bowden and the Mountaineers. "We were all shocked when Coach Bowden walked up when we were in the corner of the hotel meeting room. He sat down with us and started asking questions about the newly hired head trainer. He asked all of us our opinions of him. I felt he was using our feedback to help him see if he had made the right decision. It's a good leadership technique."

For West Virginia's center from 1974-77, Bowden's practice of listening actually served as motivation. "Coach was always willing to listen to you and give advice," said Rocky Gianola. "His demeanor and presence created an atmosphere where you did not want to fail him. It all came from the way he talked to you, treated you and supported you. Coach Bowden was like a father you couldn't let down."

Now that would be a valuable quality at Apple, IBM or your local P.T.A.

EVERYBODY WANTS TO FEEL IMPORTANT

A common desire for every person in an organization is to feel empowered. If you make your people feel like they matter you will get the very best out of them every day.

Bowden was good at it.

"I'm a high school coach and Coach Bowden did something that sticks with me to this day," said John Flath, an offensive lineman at FSU from 1990-92. "First of all, if you wrote him, he wrote you back and usually in his own handwriting. When I first started coaching, I wrote a ten page paper on my coaching philosophy. Busy as he was, coach read it and wrote me back and encouraged me to turn it into a book someday. It was such a good feeling."

B.C. Williams was an All-American offensive guard for West Virginia from 1968-72. "Coach Bowden could read people really well," he said. "I would get upset and pout sometimes. He would let you burn it off and then deal with you after you calmed down. He kind of let you work through it. Everybody liked him, but he was like a step-father to me."

Dave Van Halanger's association with Bowden stretched between his playing days at West Virginia and an 18-year stint as strength and conditioning coach at Florida State. He knows Bowden as well as anyone and his story shows a really special gift.

"One summer at Florida State I went in to see Coach to ask about a raise," said Van Halanger. "Coach's voice got real high. 'Buddy, I just don't have it in the budget, but dadgum, you're the best strength coach in the country.' I didn't get the raise but I felt like a million bucks when I left his office. Coach was terrific at empowering you to do great things. He'd see the best in you and then encourage you to go out and do it. He created an atmosphere of greatness for everyone he touched."

Empowerment is vital to the health of any person. It is important in your family, in your faith and in your profession. The lessons and observation that follow on Bowden's ability to delegate further illustrate the point.

TRUST BUT CONFIRM

People oriented leaders are never afraid to delegate.

I wrote this in the Bear Bryant book and I'll repeat it here. Many leaders think they can do the job better than anyone else, so they hesitate to delegate. They don't want to be perceived as absent on the job or not earning their paycheck. I see leaders concerned about giving too much credit to those they lead for fear of being thought of as obsolete.

Bobby Bowden was an exceptional delegator. Bowden didn't win 10 or more games for 14 years at FSU without having people he had confidence in helping him run the ship.

"When I played at West Virginia, Coach Bowden had just become head coach," said David Morris who played strong safety from 1969-73. "Coach was very green but he was wise enough to surround himself with very competent assistant coaches. He let them do their jobs which they did well."

Bowden's Florida State coaching staff would prove legendary not only for the quality of the coaches, but the fact that they all stayed together for so long and had so much success.

Defensive coordinator Mickey Andrews was the first-ever winner of the Frank Broyles Award as the nation's best assistant coach and he never left Bowden's side, retiring after 25 years on the Florida State staff.

"Not all head coaches, in fact not many head coaches, have the ability that Coach Bowden did to let his staff coach," said Andrews. "He had the ability to hire someone, tell him what he wanted and expected and then let that person go out and coach. He was not a micro-manager who was on you every minute and checking every detail of what you were doing. Bobby would give you a job to do and let you go do it."

Legendary college football announcer Brent Musburger, one of Bowden's favorites in the business I'm told, called him "the original chairman of the board. Bobby would perch up on that tower and let his assistant run things on the field below."

That image and his belief in delegation was the subject of derision by some; however, my co-writer, Rob Wilson, remembered a very high-profile coach at one of Florida State's rival schools who would offer the opinion that Bowden was merely a "figure head who didn't really coach the football team" that was a part of his regular recruiting spiel to recruits. In addition, he slipped sly comments to media members once the tape recorders had shut off. Bowden, he would suggest, did not have his head in the game and just watched aloofly from a tower.

Wilson tells me he had more than one conversation with Bowden to try and get him to throw a barb or two the other coach's way since the Seminoles were beating his team more often than not.

"No, that is just not me," said Bowden, much to Wilson's frustration at times. "You know I've just always been of the belief that what goes around, comes around to people like that."

Wilson went on to share a story that he says he's never told anyone. Some years later, the same rival coach talked in a newspaper article about how his program had gotten so big that he couldn't do everything himself and he was giving up some duties to his staff.

"I got an envelope in the mail with no stamp," said Wilson. "In it was that newspaper article about the 'innovative move' to be more of a CEO type head coach. And there was a little smiley face drawn next to the head line. I never knew who that came from and I always wondered."

Bowden's trust in putting responsibility on his assistants probably came from his history of being able to make wise choices in employees.

Casey Weldon quarterbacked the Seminoles in 1991 and 1992 and was runner-up for the Heisman Trophy as a senior. He said, "Coach Bowden clearly stated who was in charge, but he had the self-confidence to hire good people and let them do their job. He made it very clear what he expected from his staff and players and then turned them loose."

FSU's director of sports medicine throughout the majority of Bowden's 34-years in Tallahassee was Randy Oravetz. "Coach would give directions – clear and concise directions – in the staff meetings and let the assistants do their jobs. I looked upon him as the CEO of the organization, directing traffic from above," he said.

Wally Burnham coached with Bowden at FSU, went on to great success as defensive coordinator at South Florida, and is currently in the same position at Iowa State. "Coach Bowden hired people and let them do their jobs until they proved they couldn't get it done," Burnham said. "He'd let you run with your responsibilities and would step in only if you were struggling. He trusted his people and they trusted him. To be a good leader, your people have to believe in you and have confidence that you know what you are doing.

"I was the new guy on the staff in 1985, so I got stuck with being dorm supervisor. One night I had a problem so I went to see Bobby and ask him what to do. He said to me, 'I hired you to do that job, so go solve the problem.' Bobby gave me some suggestions, but he made me solve the problem. He always believed in his people."

To suggest that Bowden, or any outstanding leader, can be successful by simply throwing properly assigned tasks to his employees, family, congregation or cabinet is wrong. Leadership demands much more.

"Coach would give you everything you needed to be successful and then keep checking back with you," said Van Halanger. "When I was coaching for him, he would say 'Buddy, what can I do to help you?'"

What a powerful way for a leader to check on things. Think about all the elements that go into that question and all the answers a leader would get by asking it. With one question, which does not make the person feel he is being interrogated, Bowden found out where that coach was in getting the job done.

Jerry Johnson played defensive tackle for the Seminoles from 1996-99 and later for the Denver Broncos and he admired how Bowden handled his assistants. He said, "Coach would step in during practice and games if he felt it was necessary, but he wouldn't overstep his assistants, at least not in front of us players. Coach never felt obligated to run every aspect of the whole team, but let his assistants do their job.

"I know I read quotes from some head coaches after a game where they are beating their chests and you're like – dang – did the coach throw and catch every pass too? Coach Bowden wasn't like that."

Being willing to delegate by no means diminishes who is in charge. Bobby Bowden proved that for years.

"There was never a moment of doubt, never a single meeting when you didn't know Coach Bowden was firmly in charge," said former FSU and current Georgia assistant coach John Lilly. "Coach did a great deal of monitoring without micro-managing and there's a fine line between the two. He would let you make mistakes and he'd help cut some off, but he did it without destroying your self-respect.

"Coach never tore you down when he corrected you and he wouldn't correct you in front of your players. You never wanted to let Bobby Bowden down and fail him because he was so good to you."

Isn't it interesting to see how the ability to trust and delegate can translate in such determination in employees. This same quality can be applied to our families, our civic groups and our businesses. Lilly's observations were echoed by Jack Stanton who was an assistant for Bowden at FSU.

"Coach used to look at us in staff meetings when we were talking about a plan of attack or something," said Stanton. "He would say, 'Now, remember that you all have a vote in this and there are nine of you. But you need to remember that I always have 10 votes.'"

How about this from his own son Tommy, who would become head coach at Tulane and then, for the first time in college football history, coach against his father for nine games as Clemson's head coach? Said Tommy, "I admired his management style. He hired good assistant coaches and then gave them a sense of responsibility – coaches like that. Give 'em a job to do, hold them accountable and let 'em go. As long as Dad coached, he never had much turnover."

Delegation is a must for a great leader to be successful. Bobby Bowden figured it out very early in his career. Hire very good people, hold them accountable with clear, concise direction and let them do their jobs.

WHERE DO I STAND?

Bobby Bowden wasn't a tyrannical leader who tore around the Moore Athletic Center at Florida State daring anyone to say "no" to him.

In fact, a great leader must have the ability to be a follower when required and fall in line when and where appropriate. Two of the clearest illustrations of Bowden's ability to be a follower are linked to two of the greatest monuments of his career.

For the last six years of his career at Florida State, a statue of Bowden graced the front of the Moore Athletic Center. It is a beautiful tribute and an inspiring pose, but one that he had to be talked into. He had no interest in seeing something so grandiose erected in his honor and certainly not while he was coaching, according to several officials both inside and outside the athletic department. The Seminole Boosters were convinced that they could draw significant support dollars by selling replicas of the statue and felt that the effort had to be launched while the legend was still coaching. Reluctantly, Bowden agreed to the arrangement with the understanding that the revenue generated would go towards endowing football scholarships.

It was one of many times that Bowden went out of his way to promote FSU over his personal desires.

"We had him meeting with everybody," the late Florida State President Bernie Sliger told *The Osceola*. "If we had key faculty we needed, we'd drop in on him during the interviews. We even had him talk to some top students to try and convince them to come."

Even the naming of Bobby Bowden Field at Doak S. Campbell Stadium came sooner than the head coach would have liked. Did he slam his fist on the desk in protest when approached about the plan? No. He agreed to the arrangement, convinced by President T.K. Wetherell that it was good for his program and good for the university that the event take place sooner rather than later. Bowden eventually agreed to it, but insisted that since he had a game to coach, he would not be out there for the ceremonial unveiling. True to his word, the legendary coach was in the locker room giving his Seminoles their final words of wisdom before a game with Florida in 2004, while Ann stood at midfield with the President and 80,000 fans cheered as fireworks announced the official naming of the field.

Imagine Donald Trump refusing to watch Trump Tower unveiled because he needed to attend to his job. Or the mayor of your town skipping out on a dedication so he can make sure that the planning commission got the guidance it needed that night.

Bowden's commitment to putting Florida State University and the welfare of the whole athletic program in front of his own personal interests was admired by fund-raisers near and far.

His annual tour of Seminole booster enclaves around the south included over 35 appearances in one year alone. He was still pushing 20 stops a year in the last two years that he coached at FSU.

FOLKS WILL GIVE THEIR BEST IF THEY BELIEVE

Great leaders have a heart for people. They care about other people; they're interested in people; they have empathy for people; they love people.

Grambling's legendary football coach Eddie Robinson once said, "You got to coach every player as if he was going to marry your daughter. You can't coach 'em if you don't love 'em." Great coaches and great leaders definitely have an interest and desire to work with people. In fact, I've learned over the years if it wasn't for people, leadership would be pretty easy.

Chris Hope was a star safety for the Seminoles and is still playing in the NFL today. "I attended a Fellowship of Christian Athletes luncheon in Nashville and had not seen Coach Bowden for about ten years," he said. "I had grown a beard and I just knew he'd never remember me. He spotted me in the room and said, 'How's your mom and dad doing back in Rock Hill?' When I heard him say that, I would have signed all over again to go to Florida State."

The Wham was a powerful running play that Florida State ran extremely effectively from 1986-88 with fullback Dayne Williams carrying the ball most of the time. "To me, Coach's main leadership strength came down to one word – connection," said Williams. "He was a relationship type person, which helped build trust and confidence with his players. That made us more willing to go see him and discuss anything we were dealing with. Coach Bowden was totally genuine, everything came from his heart. Even after I left FSU, he never lost touch. He sent me a wedding gift after I'd been gone five years and he knows the names of my kids. I'm so honored by that."

Tiger McMillon played tailback at Florida State. "Coach and his staff took a personal interest in all the players," he said. "My father loved wearing boots. Coach would say, 'Tiger, how's your Dad doing? How many pairs of boots does he have now?' That showed he cared."

Tony Bryant played two years for the Seminoles and went on to a very successful career in the NFL. Later in the book he talks about having some adjustment problems, but here he shares about Bowden's team building skills.

"My high school in Marathon, Florida, a little town in the Keys, retired my jersey a few years ago," said Bryant. "Coach taped a video message and they played it in front of the whole school. I will never forget it. It brought tears to my eyes."

Clifton Abraham was a three-year starter at cornerback for Florida State and earned consensus All-America honors in 1994. He suggests Bowden went the extra mile on the team-first concept.

"Coach was great at letting guys with talent do their own thing, but he would always do it with a sense of team in mind," said Abraham. "If he thought somebody's 'showboating' hurt the team, it was over. He would have his staff room a star player with a country boy from Live Oak who was totally the opposite. That helped create good chemistry through the ranks."

You will enjoy reading about Bobby Bowden's unique ability to coach star players later on in the book.

Chapter Four:

IT'S ON THE INSIDE

"The legacy I would want is that 'he did it the right way.' I'd hate to leave a legacy that put Florida State in a bad light [and] that I ran over people. I would want my legacy to be that I did it right."

—BOBBY BOWDEN

othing puts the icing on people skills as much as character. It is imperative to effective leadership. In fact, it intertwines tightly throughout all attributes of leadership to create the strongest rope possible.

Leaders are decision-makers and many times are forced to make decisions even when they are not absolutely positive they are correct. Bobby Bowden said in his book, *The Bowden Way:* "When you don't know the answer, the surest course is to do what you believe is right. Follow your conscience. And don't take any action that you believe is morally wrong."

Character is who we are at our core. To be truly effective, leaders must be morally good at their core. Their motives must be pure, always looking out for the best interests of their followers. Such a leader has a conscience that leads to trustworthy decisions which, in turn, causes people to want to follow. They come to trust that the leader's "conscience," as Bowden puts it, will lead to the correct action.

Coach Bowden goes on to say, "I respect a person who acts with good motives. When someone lives according to high moral principles and acts in the best interest of all concerned, you can't help but admire the person, even if he is wrong."

So let's look in more detail at what Coach Bowden feels makes up a person of character.

TRUSTABILITY?

One of my favorite descriptions of what is honesty and what is integrity comes from the book *Who Moved My Cheese?* by Spencer Johnson. "Honesty is telling the truth to other people. Integrity is telling myself the truth," he writes.

In my book on Bear Bryant's leadership qualities I explain that honesty is telling the unvarnished, unleashed, unmasked truth in every situation. That doesn't mean you have to decapitate people with honesty that buries them. For example, I wouldn't tell the chairman of the board that he needs to lose a few pounds, even if he does.

A leader with integrity has a consistency to his life; he's the same person every day. I've always had the impression that Bowden was like that and it has proven true through hundreds of interviews. Coach Bowden's walk and talk always seem to be in perfect harmony.

Two thousand Heisman Trophy winner Chris Weinke was 32-3 as the starting quarterback for the Seminoles. He had played professional baseball before coming to Florida State, so he was older than his teammates and enjoyed an even deeper relationship with the coaches.

"Coach was totally honest with every player and there's no better example than that," said Weinke. "He was a role model to me when I played for him and now he's one of my best friends."

Myron Rolle is playing in the NFL for the Tennessee Titans, but that was after he took advantage of his Rhodes Scholarship to Oxford.

"What made Coach Bowden a good leader was the fact that he was steadfast to his word," said Rolle. "When I came on my visit as a high school student, he told me that he would permit me to be a true scholar athlete. The fact that he allowed me to pursue the Rhodes while being a starter on his team and miss half a game against the University of Maryland is a testament to his commitment to that promise. I think that makes him a great leader."

Sam Cowart was a consensus All-American as linebacker for the Seminoles in 1996 and was just inducted into the FSU Hall of Fame. He said, "From the time you walked through the door at FSU, Coach treated you with total honesty. He never made promises he couldn't keep, like how much playing time you'd get or making you an All-American. All he'd promise was an opportunity to do all those things, but no guarantees. I told my mother, after I got to the NFL, if I had to pick my college again, I'd go right back to FSU. Coach created a family atmosphere and I liked being a part of it."

Jamie Dukes is in the FSU Hall of Fame as an All-American offensive lineman during the early part of the Bowden dynasty. "Coach was a man of integrity and fairness," he said. "He didn't resort to lying to get you to do what he wanted. Every time he stood in front of us, we knew we were getting an honest statement. He'd never promise his recruits playing time in advance; they had to earn it."

Bowden's West Virginia players remember him for his honesty with them decades ago. "If Coach Bowden spoke it was the truth," said Chuck Smith a defensive tackle at West Virginia from 1973-76. "If he promised something or made a commitment, he delivered. He cherished his word and that's what leadership is all about. When a leader tells the truth that builds faith. Then faith develops belief and belief leads to action. I had 120 scholarship offers out of high school and Bobby Bowden was the reason I signed with West Virginia. I can't say enough about the man."

Terry Kettlewell played center at West Virginia during Bowden's last three seasons there. He said, "I respected the man for his honesty and genuineness. He was not a phony who would say one thing and then do another. You could always count on anything he told you."

You can bet that an organization that has that kind of confidence in their leadership is going to prosper. Odell Haggins has a unique frame of reference on Bowden. He was one of the all-time greats as a nose guard for the Seminoles when they began the "Dynasty Run." He won a Super Bowl ring with the San Francisco 49ers and is in his 18th season coaching with the Seminoles.

"Two words describe Coach Bowden as a leader – honesty and loyalty," Haggins said. "When I was playing, Coach came to me one day and said he needed me to switch from linebacker to the defensive line. I didn't want to do it. I was in great shape at 235-pounds, running with the backs and strong as I could get. Now Coach wanted me to move positions. I called my mom and she talked about trusting Coach. Ten minutes later I went to him to tell him I'd make the move and play nose guard. Coach said I could move to linebacker the next year.

"After the season, I went to Coach and told him I'd stay at nose guard. He was sort of surprised and asked me why? I told him it was the best way to help the team. Now, this was in 1987 and Coach said, 'Odell, one day I want you to come back and coach with me. You put other people before yourself and that's a great leadership quality.'

"After I finished my NFL career, I was working in Jacksonville completely out of football. The phone rang and it was Coach Bowden. He said he wanted me to come back to FSU and coach with him. I said, 'I don't think I could be a graduate assistant,' but Coach replied that he wanted me there full-time. It was 1994 and I've been here ever since. It all comes back to those two words I used to describe Coach Bowden as a leader – honesty and loyalty. His word is his bond."

Lawrence Dawsey earned All-America honors as a senior for the Seminoles in 1990. The star wide receiver returned to coach with his mentor and learned first-hand what he was all about. "His greatest strength as a leader was his consistency," said Dawsey. "When I played for him at FSU, I felt he was a godly man who cared about young men. Then when I started coaching for him and got behind the scenes, I saw the same godly man who disciplined young athletes and loved them unconditionally. Coach Bowden never wavered on the things he believed in."

Pat Carter played tight end for the Seminoles and for 10 years in the NFL. He said, "Coach worked you hard, but he was fair. If you did what he wanted, he'd give you an opportunity to play. He'd follow up on what he told you. Coach was a straight shooter. Not all coaches are like that. He was man of his word."

Look at how closely that observation matches what Peter McConnell, a wide receiver at West Virginia from 1975-79. He said, "Coach was so charismatic and honest with you. He meant it when he told you something and he always followed through on it."

From great players like Tamarick Vanover and Henri Crockett to FSU radio announcer Gene Deckerhoff and West Virginia offensive guard Tim Antion, Bowden's ability to tell the truth set him apart.

"I ended up at FSU because Coach won my parents over," said Florida State wide receiver Terry Anthony. "There was not one thing he told us during the recruiting process that he didn't honor. The main thing he promised me was opportunity and I'm grateful to this day."

One of the quickest ways to destroy your company, your community, your nation or a football team is to allow the seeds of distrust and suspicion to grow. It starts with the leader and for those who coached with, worked for, or played for Bowden there was never a doubt at the top.

Charlie Ward led the Seminoles to their first national championship in 1993 and won the Heisman Trophy that season. He quarterbacked the football team and also played point guard on the FSU basketball team which came within one win of making the Final Four his senior year. He is considered one of the finest all-around athletes in college history.

"When I think of Bobby Bowden as a leader I think of integrity," said Ward. "When I came out of high school, I wanted to play both football and basketball. Many coaches would promise that you could, but when a player arrives on the campus they don't deliver. They would forget all about it. Coach Bowden kept his word and allowed me to participate in both sports. However, he attached one stipulation – I had to keep my grades up. I was able to do that, so we both kept up what we had promised to each other."

Bob Goin was FSU's Athletic Director from 1990-94. "Bobby was sincere and focused on his priorities in life," said Goin. "There was nothing phony about him and people bought into that. When he told you something on Monday, it wouldn't change on Tuesday. He was consistent in his vision, values and character. You believed in Bobby. It's easy to follow a guy like that."

Former University of Florida head coach and Tennessee athletic director Doug Dickey saw the same qualities in Bowden. "Bobby was remarkably consistent in the quality of his life and the way he managed personal affairs," said Dickey. "He never wavered. He was the real thing and what he said he was, he was."

"The Coach Bowden the public knew through the media was exactly the same person we knew as players," chimed in Weinke.

"There was a total consistency with the 'coach' Bowden and the 'person' Bowden. He never wavered. His actions speak volumes about the man."

This quality was not something that emerged once his career got untracked.

"Bobby was always Bobby," said Walter Barnes who was an assistant coach at Howard College under Bowden. "He was just a genuine person with no airs about him. His boys always liked him because he told it like it was. Bobby saw it, believed it and stuck to who he was."

John Harcharic was a safety at West Virginia from 1970-74. "Coach really cared about us and was like a father figure to his players," he said. "There was nothing false or insincere about him in any way. You knew he wasn't putting on an act. The genuiness of the man was apparent to us and that made each player feel so special."

Fast forward nearly 20 years to quotes from All-American FSU punter Rohn Stark, who also had a 15-year NFL career. They are nearly identical. "Coach was the same person in private as he was to the public and the media," said Stark. "The man had only one face, never two."

Edwin Pope, one of the legendary media figures in the state of Florida, wrote for the *Miami Herald* and was quick to talk about Bowden's integrity. He told me, "As a leader, Bowden was just so solid. He had a great family background which gave him a strong foundation to build on. Bobby was a straight-on, very moral guy. And he didn't have to tell you about his strength of character, because you sensed it right away."

Florida State baseball coach Mike Martin has taken 14 Seminole teams to the College World Series and is a legend in his own right. You can hear the admiration in his voice when he talks of Bowden: "As a leader, he never changed and was just so consistent in all areas of his life. It was so refreshing to be in his presence. People are attracted to a leader like that."

"Bobby was such a genuine individual," said Chuck Amato who coached with him for 18 years before becoming the head coach at N.C. State. "He never changed who he was. One day he chewed me out, but he had a smile on his face while he was doing it. Later on I thought, 'The man just chewed me out but I didn't even know it.' But Bobby got his point across to me."

One of the games that Bobby Bowden points to as being among the most important in his FSU career was the Seminoles' 31-28 win over Nebraska in the 1987 Fiesta Bowl. The win gave FSU an 11-1 record, finishing second in the Associated Press poll. However, Bowden points to the mental hurdle it represented for his program in terms of being able to play on the biggest stage and against the best opponents.

FSU's win in that game was anything but easy and came down to one final drive. The Seminoles would have to drive 97-yards through the teeth of a great Husker defense for the come-from-behind win. Danny McManus was the FSU quarterback who had to look to the sideline for encouragement from his coach after short-arming his first pass of the drive. It was McManus who would have to trust in the play that the coaches sent in to convert a fourth down and preserve the game-winning drive.

"Coach had his priorities in order and you saw that when he recruited you," said McManus. "I went to Florida State because I knew I wanted to be a good person and I was convinced I'd be a lot better because of Coach Bowden. How you carry yourself is a key to leadership and Coach didn't change one iota no matter who he was around."

It certainly makes it easier to have confidence in that fourth down play, or that next business move, or the next hire when you have that strong foundation of trust in your leader in charge.

FSU wide receiver Randy White (1985-87) talks about the importance of words and actions working together. "I think of Coach's sincerity, his honesty and his integrity," White said. "He led by example. He was strong with words, but his deeds always followed. We had so much trust in what Coach said because he lived it. Coach Bowden was like a parent to us. You trust your parents and we trusted him. In my four years with him, I never heard him use a curse word."

Former West Virginia offensive guard Steve Early summed up what literally dozens and dozens of former players said about Bowden. He said, "Coach's character was his calling card. He led his life and as a player all you had to do was follow and you couldn't go wrong. As the years went on, all his great success didn't change him."

Trust is a quality that cannot be obtained without honesty and integrity. Bowden's intense commitment to both resulted in virtually complete trust from his teams.

"Coach Bowden made a total commitment to young men, the game of football and to his personal faith," observed Rick Stump who played offensive line for the Mountaineers from 1969-73. "As a result you could trust him completely."

Former *St. Petersburg Times* columnist Hubert Mizell may have even invented a word when asked about Bowden. He said, "Bobby had trustability if there is such a word. Parents trusted him, fans trusted him, young people trust him and that's not easy to do."

I GOT THAT

I am afraid that taking responsibility is very quickly becoming a lost quality in people and that is truly tragic. Our political system is paralyzed by "leaders" afraid that an unpopular decision might eventually cost them. There seems to be no one in Washington willing to take any real responsibility.

It is easy to take shots at politicians, but the truth is this lack of responsibility has become pervasive in our culture. At its very core, it is being insincere or maybe even dishonest, and the idea of waiting to find out the results to determine if one is going to take credit for a decision or conveniently develop "instant amnesia" is ruining us.

Clearly, Coach Bowden never leaned on the "I don't recall" method of taking responsibility, on or off the field.

"Coach would never point fingers after we lost a game," said John Eason who coached receivers at FSU. "He would say to us, 'When we lose, I take responsibility.' He would never avoid the blame in a situation and take the credit. He always took the responsibility."

Former FSU tight end Ryan Sprague, who has written his own book about his experience as a player during the 1999 season titled *Grateful,* had this to say. "I was always amazed at the incredible trust that Coach had in the men who were part of his world, especially his assistant coaches," said Sprague. "He trusted them totally, invested thoroughly in them, then stood by them. If something went wrong Coach took the blame; if it worked he handed out the credit. Coach developed leaders and then let them lead. Then the assistants invested in all of us players. It was a great system."

My co-writer, Rob Wilson, challenged me on this. "Pull up the stories on Bowden over the years and do a word-search for the number of times you find Coach Bowden using I or me after winning a game,"

Rob suggested. "Then do the same after we lost and I know you would have a dramatic illustration."

I followed Rob's advice, read all I could, and came away convinced that his point was well taken.

FSU was playing Oklahoma for the national championship in the 2000 Orange Bowl. The university had ruled All-American receiver Snoop Minnis out of the game by institutional rule. He was eligible to play, but a procedural interpretation by the school meant he couldn't play. And the departure of Mark Richt to Georgia and the uncertainty of who might join him left an unusually unsettled climate during bowl preparation.

The Seminoles played very poorly offensively in the game and suffered a heart-breaking loss that allowed a host of opportunities to slip through the program's fingers.

As usual, Bowden appeared before the press following the game and got drilled about the FSU loss from the packed room stuffed with national reporters. He took full responsibility for the damaging loss and repeatedly turned away opportunities to point blame at his staff or players. He looked tired and disheartened when he left the podium.

On the way to the team buses, Rob Wilson was talking with one of the assistant coaches who was shaking his head. "We should have listened to Coach," he admitted. "All week Coach was saying that he had the feeling this was going to be a 'between the tackles' game for us. He kept encouraging us to think about running the ball right up the gut. 'Hit 'em in the nose,' he said, which wasn't usually his first choice. We all talked him out of it. I think the old Bull was right."

Never once in any of the interviews following a game did Bowden ever take the opportunity to suggest, "My plan might have worked if they had just listened." He never berated players for their performance nor coaches for their decisions. He let the loss rest with him.

Bobby Bowden's sense of responsibility is something he imparted to his players and staff.

Mark Ruckman was a linebacker at West Virginia who graduated in 1970. "My senior year my mom died," he said. "I was down and felt depressed and started to slack off in my winter workouts and studies. Coach brought me in and basically kicked my tail. He told me that life moves on and I need to get with it quickly. He told me to take care of my responsibilities because my mother would want that. 'Do it for her,' Coach said. For the rest of my life I've taken responsibility for my actions. When things get me down, I have to pick myself up and keep moving. I've had a long career with Time Warner and I owe much of that to the lessons Coach taught me at West Virginia."

Listen to this story from former West Virginia graduate assistant Bob Antion.

"I was just a scrub player at Penn State but I wanted to go into coaching," said Antion. "That wasn't going to happen at Penn State, so I went to West Virginia to get a chance. In the fall of 1974 I arrived in Morgantown as a graduate assistant, but I got there late and there were no positions really open for me. Coach Bowden told me I could be a dorm counselor until I could become a fulltime G.A.

"I moved in the dorm early before the counselors and started going to fall practice. Pretty soon, the rest of the counselors arrived and the head counselor invited me to attend a welcome back picnic. It was an invitation, not a mandate, as I understood it. I didn't attend the picnic and went to practice that evening. The next morning I was fired for not attending. In addition, that same night I had loaned someone my car and the guy totaled it. So on that one night I lost my job, my spot to live, and my car.

"Needless to say I was devastated. I was in tears thinking I'd have to go home as a total failure and embarrassment. I called Coach Bowden at his home and told him what had happened. Coach said, 'Meet me after practice and we'll go over to First National Bank.' He set up an account, Bobby Bowden Enterprises, and he wrote me a check for $1,000 to go get a place to stay.

"I asked Coach about my master's tuition and he paid for that as well. He also told me I could eat my meals at the athletes' training table. Then he called the local Ford dealer and bought me a car. I had known this man for less than a week."

WHEN YOU'RE AT WORK, WORK

A leader must have an intense work ethic if he is going to be successful. If a leader is lazy, then he's not a leader.

Coach Bowden was driven by his determination to be as successful as he possibly could on the football field. He was as intense, focused and hard-nosed when attacking his work as the most well-known task masters, but he managed to keep that all-important life balance in place. His own son, Jeff, who coached with his dad for ten years, said his dad preached a timeless message.

He told me, "Dad was able to adjust and adapt to the different generations and get his message across because it was timeless. He was communicating four prime principles – faith, commitment, work ethic and responsibility: I think there are times when people on the outside did not get an appreciation for how hard Coach worked, or how hard he drove his players. He was tough and he demanded toughness."

Bowden talked about that with Christian Klemash in the book *How to Succeed in the Game of Life*. "Number one, when you get a job, treat it like it's the last job you'll ever have," he said. "Work like it's the last day you'll have on Earth, and do the absolute best that you can. A lot of guys get in a position and start looking for their next job. 'Where can I get a better job? How can I get promoted?' Things like that. Just do the best you can, and give it everything you've got and that other stuff will take care of itself."

Doing your best becomes a constant theme as you examine Bowden as a leader. "You can only do your best," he told Klemash. "Let's put doing your best ahead of winning. Just do the best you can do, that's all you can do. I hammer that a lot to my players."

Former Florida State president T.K. Wetherell was a wide receiver under Bobby Bowden when he was an assistant at Florida State in the '60s. He later became his boss at the end of his career. He told me, "He could really inspire people with his energy and never seemed to tire. Coach put in extremely long hours, outworked everyone and visited all the booster clubs all over Florida. It was amazing to watch him in action."

Earlier in this book Lou Holtz complemented Bowden by saying that his teams "always played loose." Part of that comes from Bowden's belief that players and coaches can only control so much: "Do your individual very best and let the rest take care of itself."

Dan Mowrey was the FSU kicker from 1991-94. "Coach's philosophy was to prepare yourself, work hard, and then win or lose," said Mowrey. "You can sleep well at night because you know you gave it your all. Then the next day you're ready to fight again. Coach was all about the drive to get better."

Even Bowden fans may be surprised at how intense he could get. He clearly believed that football was a demanding game and at the core believed that the strongest and toughest team would win. This comes from his "state of the union" address in 2009: *Coaches must build confidence, enthusiasm, meanness and toughness.*

Bowden famously challenged his Seminoles at halftime of a game against Florida in 1986. He had allowed a documentary of the entire season to be filmed and the cameras were rolling when an incensed

Bobby paced in front of the team. "Are you scared?" asked Bowden in a strained yell. "Are you scared out there? Is there something about their colors that has got you scared?" Bowden knew that it was time to challenge their manhood. He could be intense.

Because Bowden was so organized and meticulous, we get a fascinating inside look at what he demanded. Here is an excerpt from a document Bowden delivered to his coaches. He has a hand-written note in the margin to credit Dick Vermeil of the St. Louis Rams.

> *Your responsibilities will be delegated to you. Don't look for anyone to cover for you in anything you've been assigned to do.*
>
> *The morale of a football team is a direct reflection of its coaching staff, so it is imperative that the players see us as a group who care about each other.*
>
> *Every once in a while, review your job description. Don't delete or reassign responsibilities. If anything, add to them.*
>
> *Always work to improve. You are going to be held responsible for the performance of your position.*

Bowden says, "When at work…work!"

THEY'LL TEST YOU

Perseverance is a quality that leads to success in any professional field. If you're a plumber, a counselor or the President, there will be times when you're feeling discouraged. A leader must persevere. If you as a leader don't persevere, how can you expect your troops to? If you quit, what will keep your employees from doing the same?

The entire nation watched Bobby Bowden persevere in 2004.

The Bowden family had just finished a birthday celebration for namesake grandson Bowden Madden at Bobby and Ann's Tallahassee home. Madden was the 15-year old son of daughter Ginger and ex-husband and former FSU player John Madden. Ginger was going to spend the weekend at her parent's home, but John and Bowden set out for the two hour drive to Ft. Walton Beach with a hurricane looming just a few hours away.

Florida Highway Patrol reports showed that the car the two were traveling in crossed the median on Interstate 10 and crashed head-on into a truck, killing both John and Bowden. Ann Bowden, would pour some of her grief into painstaking research to discover the cause of the accident, including personal interviews with witnesses, which she believes was the result of a hurricane generated wind gust that swept the car off track.

Football suddenly seemed very small to the Bowden family and the FSU football team. In a cruel twist of fate, it was September 2004 and the Seminoles were opening the season at Miami in just six days.

Bowden had to lead his team all week while battling numbing grief. Punter Chris Hall remembered that awful time. He said, "Coach remained even keeled through every storm he encountered and that all related to his life and faith. He always let God work things out and as a result never got too high or too low. I remember when he lost his relatives in the accident. He spoke to us and told us what needed to be said. He held himself together even though he was suffering deeply. He kept things in perspective which was a positive example to us in how to handle adversity."

Bowden sat in his hotel room the night before Florida State would take on the Hurricanes and wrote each of his children hand-written letters until deep into the night. Author Mike Freeman published one of the letters in *Bowden*, and the power and strength of a man and his faith has never been better illustrated. Florida State lost in overtime at Miami in a battle of teams ranked No. 4 and No. 5, but sports fans got a lesson in what leadership is all about.

The Tampa Tribune's Joe Henderson gave this account of that difficult time: "I covered FSU for five seasons at the front end of the Bowden era. But the leadership example of Coach Bowden that sticks in my mind was in 2004 well after I was covering the team regularly. It came following the death of his grandson and former son-in-law in a car accident.

"The funeral was on the day before FSU went to Miami to play the Hurricanes. I was dispatched to Miami, specifically to cover how Bowden was handling things. What I saw was an amazing show of strength and leadership that I still marvel at.

"FSU had the game in hand, but stumbled down the stretch and lost in overtime. Bowden shook hands with Miami coach Larry Coker then walked off the field alone. Players later commented about how Bowden never mentioned his personal grief before or after the game. But they clearly knew he was hurting.

"He met the media afterward and mumbled some stuff about the game, but I could see his heart wasn't in it. How could it be? After that, I pulled him aside for a few questions and he admitted, 'It was hard for my mind not to be somewhere else.'

"I moved on and began to interview players and coaches and Bowden drifted off to tend to other responsibilities. About ten minutes later, I heard my name called and turned to see Bobby Bowden about fifteen feet away. He flipped the hat he had worn during the game to me and said simply, 'Give it to your grandson.'

"I don't have a grandson yet, but the hat has a proud place on my mantle. One day I'll tell a grandson about this man, Bobby Bowden, and how a real leader handles adversity."

"There is adversity involved in everything," Bowden told Christian Klemash in the book *How to Succeed In The Game of Life.* "I'll never forget the first head coaching job I had. I was 25-years-old and head coach at South Georgia College. We won our first game and then our second game. All of a sudden I'm thinking I might not ever lose a game. 'Man, I am the answer to the coaching profession.' We played the next game and got beat 61 to about 20 and now I'm beginning to wonder if I ought to even be in coaching.

"And I've been on the verge of quitting, but what else would I rather do? I'd rather do this than anything in the world. So we stay with it, but there's been three or four times in my career where I was faced with the thought of quitting and each time I'd say, 'I'd rather do this than anything else' and that's how I got through adversity."

How important is the trait of perseverance to Bobby Bowden? Just two words appeared on a sign that he had his players walk through to the practice fields every day at Florida State. On the way in it read PERSEVERANCE and on the way out it read ENTHUSIASM.

MIGHT BE TOUGH TO SWALLOW

There is the sense that to be successful in college football a head coach must be a dominating personality whose very presence sucks all the air out of a room. He's got to have a bigger than life ego and demand homage at every turn.

That may well be the stereotype these days, but it is not the man we study in this book and it's not the quality of the great leaders that I've come to know.

West Virginia linebacker Mark Euopolus played from 1971-75 and he said it better than I can: "Coach Bowden proves that you don't have to be a bad guy to be a great leader. So many leaders feel they have to be rough, tough and abrasive to be effective. Coach motivated without that heavy hand. He was a humble guy who never put himself in the spotlight. He always wanted the focus to be on his players, the assistant coaches and the team."

Bowden's humble nature is one of the qualities that is easiest to recognize and the most surprising to those who don't know him. FSU students were shocked when he would drive up on the first tee of the Seminole Golf Course and ask, "Do you need a fourth?"

Once stuck in the Atlanta airport, Bowden saw two gals (as he always calls them) with FSU t-shirts at the gate debating on what to do after they had learned the flight to Tallahassee was canceled. A few minutes later it was Bowden, the two FSU coeds and a philosophy major renting a small car and driving through the night to reach Tallahassee.

Rob Wilson tells of the time when he and coach landed at the private air strip in Tallahassee. As Rob was driving off, he saw Coach Bowden walking across the huge field towards the main terminal holding up his suit pants so the sandspurs wouldn't stick to them.

"Coach, can I give you a ride?" yelled Wilson realizing Bowden's car was parked at the main lot. "Nah, it can't be more than a half mile," said Bowden waiving him off.

Longtime FSU assistant coach Jim Gladden suggests that humility was Bowden's greatest asset: "He'd say to us, 'If you ever big league it with some high school coach you are visiting, I won't support you. If that coach wants to sit and talk with you for three hours, you sit there with him and listen.'"

Ed Pastilong was West Virginia's recruiting coordinator in 1975. "Bobby generated immediate respect from people when they encountered him," said Pastilong. "He was just enjoyable to be around because he was easy to work with. He's a big, important football coach, but he's always been just Bobby to everyone. You never felt you were in the presence of a celebrity. You were just with Bobby."

Even his boss at Florida State was struck by the quality. "Bobby never allowed success to change him despite all of his success," said former FSU Athletic Director Dave Hart. "His core values remained unchanged and his concern for people from all levels of society was always consistent. I first met Bobby in 1971 when he was an assistant coach at West Virginia and many years later I saw the same at FSU when he'd become one of the greatest football coaches of all time. Through all the years and all the good and bad times, I never heard anyone ever say, 'Bobby is just not the same guy he used to be.' "

Dave Van Halanger played four years for Bowden at West Virginia and then worked with him for 18 more as an assistant at FSU. He said, "The man never changed. It was never about Bobby Bowden. It was about God, his players, his family, FSU. His ego never played into it."

His humility worked well in the recruiting world as well. Thomas Loadman was a backup quarterback at West Virginia from 1973-77. "He didn't posses an ounce of arrogance," Loadman said. "That was a huge help to him as a super recruiter. When he came to my house my mom baked a pie. He told her it was the best he ever tasted and she just fell in love with him that day."

Derrick Brooks is one of the greatest linebackers in the history of college football and a shoe-in for the NFL Hall of Fame as well. He was a two-time consensus All-American for the Seminoles in 1993 and 1994. He was one of the most heavily recruited players in the nation as the *USA Today* high school player of the year, but it may have been Bowden's humility that turned him to FSU.

He said, "Coach came to my house to visit and it was just so comfortable. Here he was talking away and talking really more about Florida State as a school than as a football program. He explained what the academic opportunities were and how much an education meant. Then he starts into the football part of it and my little sister crawls up in his lap and falls asleep while he's talking. He doesn't miss a beat, just puts his arm around her and talks about the future. That was it."

The key to his humility? It was not an act and not reserved just for the budding super stars. "Many years after my time at West Virginia I went down to Florida to attend a reunion that was honoring Coach Bowden," said Bob Pitrolo, who was head manager from 1972-76. "We were in a little banquet hall at the Gator Bowl and Coach recognized me even though he didn't remember my name. He came out to speak to me, which still remains one of my most precious memories."

Beloved is the executive, principal or priest who recognizes they aren't better than anyone else in the room.

WE ARE TALKING DOWN THE ROAD SMARTS

Influencing the people under you is really the only way to lead. You can talk leadership and teach leadership, but at the end of the day, you lead by your influence, not your authority. I suspect Coach Bowden will be surprised by the depth of his leadership influence.

"I never will forget the meeting we had in 1993 before the National Championship game," said Andre Wadsworth who was the quintessential FSU defensive end and earned consensus All-America honors in 1997 before becoming the highest drafted FSU player ever as the third pick of the Arizona Cardinals. "The whole squad was together on the eve of the game. Coach said, 'There will never be a time like this again when we're gathered like this. I'm going to speak to you as if you were my own sons.' He then proceeded to address us on the issue of morals and ethics, not football. He warned us about pre-marital sex, partying, alcohol and drugs, he covered everything without a word about the national championship or even the game the next day. That was it.

"You see, as a leader your job is to influence others. That's what leadership is. Coach Bowden didn't ever squander the leadership responsibilities he possessed."

Christian Ponder was Bowden's last starting quarterback and was drafted in the first round by the Minnesota Vikings in 2011. "He was unbelievable to play for," said Ponder. "It was a dream for me to play for him. My dad played for him back in the early eighties. It was just the way that he treats guys not only on the field but off the field. You realize he is one of the best coaches in college football history on the field, but off the field he has helped so many guys become men and changed their lives completely. He influenced my dad who in turn influenced me. Obviously, he is going to go down as one of the greatest."

Richard Goodman is in his second year as a wide receiver with the San Diego Chargers. "Coach has one model and he sticks to it," he said. "He always told us it's all about going out there and doing your best. He would point out that everyone on the roster is a man and everyone is here for a reason. It's similar to what Coach (Norv) Turner says here about representing your name on the back of the jersey. Coach Bowden would tell us how important it is to represent the spear on our helmet."

Bobby Jackson was an All-American halfback at Howard College in 1962 who went on to become a college coach and an assistant in the NFL. "Bobby Bowden was the first Christian man I had ever been around." Jackson confessed. "I had never met one before. Coach didn't pound his beliefs down your throat. He just lived his faith and that made a lasting impression on me."

Clay Shiver earned All-America honors at center on FSU's national championship team 31 years after Jackson played at Howard. He said,

"My life in ministry is a direct result of Coach Bowden's spiritual investment in my life. I can trace my Christian walk right back to the seeds he planted in my soul when I was at FSU. He did that with hundreds of his players over all those years of coaching."

"I was the head coach at Salem College when Coach Bowden hired me in 1970 to be the head freshman coach at West Virginia," said Donnie Young. "I was loud and rough on the kids, so halfway through the season Coach pulled me into his office. He said, 'Donnie, you need a change of attitude out there.' He explained to me that you've got to find that thin line between being too tough and too easy. He wanted me to be somewhere in the middle. That meeting changed my approach to coaching and I'm still at it over 40 years later."

FSU baseball coach Mike Martin says "He epitomized what John Maxwell states in his books, 'Leadership is influencing; nothing more, nothing less.' Bobby Bowden influenced everyone he came in contact with, especially other coaches and players."

Running back Bob Gresham was one of the first black players at West Virginia from 1967-70. He said, "I didn't have a father figure in my life, so Coach took over that role. I looked upon him as my Dad. Even though I was one of his first black athletes, he'd still say to me, 'Hey, boy,' which I didn't view as disrespectful but rather that I was one of his kids. He was such a great person."

Gene McDowell was FSU's first All-America football player in the early '60s and became an assistant coach for the Seminoles. He later served as head coach at the University of Central Florida and remains close to the FSU program today. Gene told me, "Any leader must set the example and that was Bobby's strongest quality. He influenced all of us about how to live your life, the importance of being involved in the FCA, and possessing a strong work ethic."

Charlie Ward, who once told FSU basketball coach Pat Kennedy that he "didn't have to yell" during a timeout in an overtime game, agreed with the lasting influence of Coach Bowden on his life. "There was no ranting, no raving and no curse words. That aspect of Coach's style has stayed with me all these years," said Ward.

Bill Ragans was a hard-hitting safety for the Seminoles from 1987-90. He said, "Coach didn't just tell us how to act, he showed us. If we messed up he'd sit you down and have a good talk with you. Coach did as much fathering as he did coaching. He discussed religion, your path in life, what it takes to be a real man, etc. He was coaching life as much as football."

Chris Hope was as outstanding in the classroom as he was as a safety on the football field. The Tennessee Titan said, "Coach never told us to do something he wasn't already doing. Many leaders don't follow what they are saying. Coach always led by example, by the way he conducted himself. That's the best kind of leadership."

"We were all watching to see how he conducted himself and how he held himself up," admitted Greg Jones who led the Seminoles in rushing in 2001, 2002 and 2003 and is in his seventh year with the Jacksonville Jaguars. "As a young player, I began to think, 'When I get older I want to be like Coach Bowden and conduct my life just like he does.' That's the power of a leader's influence."

ABC Announcer Brent Musburger took the scene back to that recruiting living room: "Bobby was outstanding with families. When it was time to close on a high school kid, Bobby would visit the home to wrap things up. His religious beliefs and high standards meant a lot to mothers. They wanted their sons to be associated with a man like Bobby."

Seven-year NFL veteran and former Seminole great Dedrick Dodge (1986-89) appreciated the Bowden approach. He said to me,

"I view Coach as a great leader because of his demeanor which came from his Christian values. He didn't have to yell and cuss at us. It was his demeanor that demanded our respect."

Perhaps we should let ESPN's Lee Corso sum up Bobby Bowden as a leader.

"Bobby was exactly what he was," said Corso who has known him since 1951. "He was always Bobby Bowden and that gave him credibility as a great leader. He was an original and didn't try to be someone he wasn't. As a result, he was always well respected by his players because they knew he believed in what he was saying. His teams always had faith in their coach. When a team thinks their coach is a phony, you're dead. Through all the struggles of life, Bobby was always himself. For 81 years, he has been true to who he is. He's never wavered."

Chapter Five:

YOU HAVE TO KNOW YOUR STUFF

"Here my old man is 63 years old that year, and he's deciding if he
can change and do something first before somebody else so he can win a
national championship. And it won him a national championship."
—TERRY BOWDEN

believe that all the seven elements (Vision, Communication Skills, People Skills, Character, Competence, Boldness, Serving Heart) are in place in all effective leaders.

However, the one dimension – the one component – the single quality that no leader can be successful without is competence. Competence by dictionary definition is: *possession of required skill, knowledge, qualification or capacity.* Whether your strongest skills lie in communications, or boldness, or vision, without competence you won't last long. Leaders must be good – really good – at what they do.

I encourage you to read *How Bobby Bowden Forged a Dynasty* by Mike Freeman. In the book, Freeman relays the following story which came as a surprise even to those closest to Bowden, and illustrates just what kind of a football coach he was.

A former college coach now an NFL assistant was asked by Freeman just how good Bowden was as a coach.

"The best way to answer that is with a story not even Bobby knows about," said the coach who asked not to be identified. "Our team cheated against Florida State, and we still couldn't beat him. We cheated badly, and that _____ still won.

"Bobby's team was coming to play us (the coach gives a time frame of only 'the last two decades' to remain anonymous) and we were scared to death of Florida State. They were killing teams…they were very intimidating.

"So we did some things I regret to this day. One thing we did was send someone to spy on his practices. We saw a lot of their plays and what they were planning to do. Mainly we saw some of the trick plays they were practicing. We got tons of information.

"Then we put microphones in the visitor's locker room of our stadium. We heard just about everything before the game and at halftime [that] Florida State was planning. At halftime we listened in to what Bobby told the team. We knew some of the plays they were going to run. Bobby and his assistants were talking about some defensive stuff too. We stole a bunch of stuff.

"I would guess we knew probably 30 or 40 percent of what they were going to do based on cheating like that. It might have been more. But you know what? We still lost.

"So how good a coach is Bowden? We had some pretty good players on our team when we faced him. Our coaches were cut-throat (blanks) with no conscience, and we were good. We

spied on his practices. We wired his locker room like we were the _____ CIA. We did all that, and he still beat us. I thought after that, 'This is the greatest coach I've ever seen.'

"People don't give Bobby enough credit for being very smart and a great tactical coach."

I salute Freeman for digging up an amazing story and give a tip of the cap towards Bowden for what is clearly a mastery of his profession. Looking deeper into his competence it is clear that he was uniquely suited to become college football's second all-time winningest coach.

"The Florida State player that everybody thinks of when they talk about the end zone prancing is Deion Sanders," Bowden told Ben Brown for the book, *Winning's Only Part of the Game.* "And he's a pretty good example of how people misread a player's style as some indication of disrespect for the game. I don't think I've ever had a player who had more love or respect for football than Deion and I can't think of many who were more admired by coaches and teammates.

"Around the players, Deion never played the star. That was for public consumption. I've had great players who would do just about anything they could to avoid practice. But Deion never asked out of anything. Deion was going to put on a show on Saturdays, and as long as he wasn't breaking any rules, I wasn't about to do anything to take away from the enthusiasm be brought to our team."

Bowden's affection for one of his brightest stars was mutual. "He will always be Coach Bowden to me," said Sanders. "By that I mean I wouldn't ever call him Bobby and I don't like it when I hear the media or even former players call him Bobby. It will always be Coach Bowden to me. I love him. And the best way to put it is that I think he was the greatest college football coach ever. Ever!"

"Bobby was a guy anointed from birth to lead," said Edwin Pope who was the highly acclaimed columnist for the *Miami Herald* for years. "I picture him as always leading – in front of the class, at the head of the line, or leading down the field. I can't picture Bobby in a subordinate position, but always on top.

"Bobby was born to win and I felt that way about him from the very first day I met him. I had a speaking engagement in Douglas, Georgia at a banquet when Bobby was coaching at South Georgia College. I'd never heard of the school or their coach, but I remember Bobby as an impressive guy. I knew he'd be big for a long time. He was destined for big things."

Bennie Storey was a Little All-American for Bobby Bowden at Howard College. He put it pretty simply when he told me, "He was always thorough and diligent. We were always well-prepared. We might get beaten but we were never outcoached."

While I remain one of Edwin Pope's biggest fans and deeply respect the man, I seriously doubt that any leader is born with the skills it takes to lead. I've checked the Orlando newspaper every day for the headline that reads, "Great natural leader born yesterday at Florida Hospital!" I haven't seen that headline yet, so I've come to the realization that leaders can be developed.

Coach Bowden didn't see himself as a natural leader. He told me, "As a young athlete and student, I never thought of myself as a leader. In a group setting, someone might 'volunteer' me as a spokesman. I'd get put into a leadership role, so I guess others saw it before I understood what was going on."

I suppose some leaders burst from the delivery room ready to lead without any training, experience or background, but they would be very, very few. I am convinced that leadership skills can be developed and enhanced. We can all be better leaders. If not, you can just wipe out a whole section of books at your local store. You can just about clear the shelves in three rooms of my house. And why would you be reading this book?

Let's hear what a Rhodes Scholar thinks of Bowden's qualifications as a leader. I remember the ESPN footage of Myron Rolle arriving late to the FSU at Maryland game because he had to complete his interview in front of the Rhodes Scholarship committee earlier that day. "I think his greatest strength was understanding each individual personality of his team and his coaching staff," said Rolle. "For me, my emphasis was on academics, community involvement and being an outstanding athlete. For other guys it might have been growing closer to God and being an outstanding athlete. For other guys it might have been using Coach Bowden as a father figure because they didn't have one at home. He understood his players and coaching staff. As a leader you really have to be in touch with the people you lead and he certainly was that."

Remember back when Bobby Bowden talked about his father telling him that he was "just as good as anybody else!" Does that sound like a message delivered by a father to his natural born leader son? Coach Bowden learned how to be a leader who would win seven national Coach of the Year honors. You can learn how to be a better leader as well.

Bowden's former boss at West Virginia puts it pretty simply. "Bobby Bowden's best leadership skill is that he got the job done. That's what a leader is supposed to do, isn't he?" suggested former athletic director Leland Byrd.

Doc Weiss was a fullback at West Virginia from 1966-69. He said, "Coach was my position coach so I never played for him as a head coach. We didn't have a lot of great players back them, but he was always innovative. He wanted to put the ball in the air and score points. We all knew he had a great football mind."

It's time to look at what we can learn from Coach Bowden, whose competence in the area of college football coaching is undeniable.

PROBLEMS NEVER GET EASIER

General Colin Powell, our former U.S. Secretary of State, said this: "Leadership is solving problems. When people stop bringing you their problems, you're through as a leader."

Just how intense this "problem solving" element of the job was for Bobby Bowden might best be illustrated by quotes he is giving now in retirement. "Every day is Saturday," said Bowden recently. "There are no phone calls about this, no meetings about that, no time table for a decision on this. I don't have to worry about what I'm going to learn next about one of my players. I'm not worried about some of the issues they may be facing at home. No one is running grades across my desk." You get the impression that Bowden doesn't miss those elements of the job, but his ability to solve problems helped make him a great leader.

Former FSU and Denver Bronco defensive lineman Jerry Johnson had similar thoughts. "He was a father figure away from home for his players," he echoed. "I always felt comfortable walking into his office, because I could talk to him about anything."

Rick Stockstill played quarterback for Bowden at FSU in the late 1970s and is now the head coach at Middle Tennessee State University. He told me, "Coach was always so honest with us and communicated so clearly. He was accessible. You could always go in and visit at his office. As a result he instilled a high level of confidence in us. He'd motivate a good player to be great and a great player to be all-world."

Keith Jones played on some of the all-time great Seminole defenses of 1979 and '80. "Coach used to tell us to 'just chip away at the rock.'" remembers Jones who went on to call FSU games for Sun Sports for 20 years. "He was teaching us to just keep at it, one day at a time. You can't get everything done all at once. Be patient and keep working away every day."

Bill McKenzie played for Bowden at West Virginia twenty years before Johnson played for him at FSU yet look at what he said: "You were always his son no matter when or where you played for him. I could always go in and talk to him and seek his advice on any topic. Coach always had time for me."

Coach Bowden's problem solving skills clearly revolved around an ability to communicate personally with those he met with and counseled.

"Coach made each individual feel that you were the most important person in the world at that moment when he was dealing with you," said FSU's tight end from 1990-94 Lonnie Johnson who would go on to play six years in the NFL. "The information he shared with you was exactly what he'd be telling his own children."

Sam Childers also played tight end for Bowden at FSU, but he was one of his first Seminole recruits in the late 1970s. "Coach was honest and he had integrity," he told me. "He was convinced in what he was saying and you believed it because whenever he spoke you knew it was the truth. You could always ask him for help."

GET OUT THERE AND SELL DADGUMIT

The company that doesn't have every employee thinking about selling their product is the company that is not going to reach its potential.

One sports team I read about has a motto that says, "We are all the ticket office." You have got to be engaged in the sales effort. The best salesperson in any organization must be the leader at the top. He sets the tone for everyone else.

You want a salesman? How about Bobby Bowden, who convinced players to sign with Florida State when they had won just four games over the previous three seasons? What if I let you in on the secrets of a guy who convinced players that they could win with a schedule that read at Nebraska, at Ohio State, at Notre Dame, at Pitt and at LSU! How good a salesman was Bowden when he had the program rolling and had to convince high school All-Americans that it would be better for them to come to FSU and wait to play rather than going to play right away at another school?

It is hard to believe now, but in the early 1980s it was hard to draw much interest in the FSU vs. Miami game, which would grow to become the dominate rivalry in college football during the 1990s. Bowden was very fond of then Hurricane head coach Howard Schnellenberger and still considers him one of the "finest coaches I ever coached against." In an effort to drum up interest, the two head coaches agreed to a press conference the week before the game. They squared off in a boxing ring complete with gloves to mug for the cameras and talk about the game.

"It was really unbelievable," said Wayne Hogan who was the creative FSU Sports Information Director at the time. "We knew that the two liked each other, but really didn't think they would agree to it. There was Howard smoking his pipe and Bowden swinging a low blow. It was public relations gold."

Coach Schnellenberger told me that, "Bobby had a soft-sell approach to leadership. You didn't see Bobby raise Cain very often. He was more of a soft-sell kind of guy, which made him a great recruiter."

Earlier in the book we learned about Coach Bowden "selling" current FSU assistant coach Odell Haggins on moving from his starting linebacker position to nose guard. Brent Musburger talked about how if "Bobby got to Mama it was all over." And countless players talked about how great Bowden's skills were as a recruiter.

Anquan Boldin is one of the top receivers in the NFL and was the subject of a huge recruiting battle. He told me that he still talks to Coach Bowden frequently even though he's an All-Pro now. "Coach Bowden was the person who clinched my decision to attend Florida State," said Boldin who starred at FSU from 1999-2002. "When he recruited me, he walked into my house like he had been there a hundred times before. The comfort level he established and his ability to inspire was evident from the beginning. I quickly knew I wanted to play for him.

"I think his strongest quality was how he instilled hope and confidence in guys. I think everybody who came through Florida State had a belief that they were the best player in that program. That comes straight from the top in Coach Bowden. He always had his finger on the pulse of the team and understood how he could maximize our potential."

Letroy Guion wears a Minnesota Vikings uniform now, but he used to sit in Bobby Bowden's locker room. "Coach Bowden told me the truth about football," he said. "He taught me how to play the game of football, and taught us all how to approach a game. Our mindset was that we are going to win right off the bat."

Sometimes a great salesperson's reputation precedes them. Current University of Georgia assistant coach and former FSU recruiting coordinator John Lilly once told my co-writer of a cross country visit: "We had a bunch of assistants all stuffed in this little plane and were flying out to Los Angeles to meet with a recruit that one former NFL coach said could play in the league right out of high school. Coach really didn't like to recruit too far from the South unless the player was "a difference-maker" as he would tell us.

"So Coach is kind of challenging me on whether we were flying all the way out there for nothing. He pointed out that USC and UCLA were right down the road for the kid. Anyway, we stuff ourselves into a van and are headed for his street. We turn the corner – in Los Angeles mind you – and the entire block, maybe 25 houses, are decked out in hand made FSU signs. People are having bar-b-ques on their front lawns and waving 'We Love Bobby' signs. It was unreal. Coach just kind of laughed and said, 'I feel good about this one.'"

One key to Bowden's coaching longevity was that he never got tired of recruiting. He never stopped selling.

"I really enjoyed recruiting all along," said Bowden. "I know that a lot of coaches get to seeing it as a bother and I just never have. I enjoy people and maybe that is the key. I liked meeting the young men and their families and I believed in what I was selling. I felt as though they would be missing out on an education from Florida State. The actual traveling could get tiring, but I never lost my energy for recruiting."

Bobby Jackson was an All-American halfback at Howard College from 1959-62 and he went on to coach in both college and the NFL. He said, "Back in our Howard days, none of us were smart enough to know what we had in Coach Bowden. He was special."

Bobby Bowden was always selling…selling a school, a playbook, a philosophy, a chance for success, a path for a victorious life.

LISTEN AND SILENT USE THE SAME LETTERS

I have written two books about John Wooden and I illustrated in each that throughout his legendary career Wooden never used the word "coach." It was always "teach," "teacher," and "teaching."

I am a huge proponent of a being a life-long learner. The truly great people that I have been privileged to come in contact with over my lifetime or studied from afar have this trait in common. They continue to strive to learn as much as they can about the subjects that interest them. You can't teach unless you're committed to be a learner.

The reason is that the world is changing so fast therefore, you must be on the cutting edge of learning every day.

Bobby Bowden is a lifelong learner. He's a tremendous historian of World War II. He's read a room full of books on the subject and has studied the personalities and skills of the great military leaders from both sides. A few years ago an *ESPN Magazine* photographer was allowed to spend 24 hours with Bowden for a photo montage. The most striking image is the one taken from the fairway of the golf course behind his home. He is sitting in a big old bath robe at the kitchen table at 5:30 in the morning reading his Bible. He has done this virtually his whole life.

Here is a man who first preached in a church in 1953 when the minister grabbed him as a volunteer youth pastor and asked him to fill in. He's not reading Scripture every morning to register on the heavenly scoreboard. He is still learning and growing stronger as a Christian leader.

At age 81, Bowden remains a voracious reader of history and continues to collect stories that he can include in public speaking opportunities.

He was a great learner as a coach as well. I was told by a number of his coaches that Bowden was at his roots a "three yards and a cloud of dust" type coach. What? The guy who called the Puntrooskie? The same guy who had Casey Weldon throw to Charlie Ward (who had slipped in at wide receiver) who threw back to Weldon down the sideline at Michigan in 1991? That guy?

"Coach believed in taking what the defense gave you," admitted 2000 Heisman Trophy winner Chris Weinke. "He wouldn't go into a week of practice determined to win the game his way. He would go in determined to win it period. He told me once that if we could win a game by running the fullback up the middle on every single play that he would be happy as he could be. I really believe the passing game and the trick plays just gave him the best chance to win."

Peter Tom Willis quarterbacked what may have ended up being FSU's best offense ever in 1989 although the season didn't start that way. The Seminoles lost their first two games then rallied to win ten in a row over the likes of LSU, Auburn, Miami and Florida and finished with a 41-17 trouncing of Nebraska in the Fiesta Bowl. Willis told Rob Wilson once about his first meeting with Bobby Bowden.

"I was from Alabama so I knew all about Coach Bowden and I was just so excited to be there," Wilson recounted Willis saying. "Here I was at FSU and just a freshman so I knew I wasn't in the mix so to speak, but I couldn't wait for that first meeting with THE Coach Bowden. Coach walked up in front of us quarterbacks and drew a stick figure on the board. Then he drew another stick figure on the other side of the board. He drew a dashed line in a big loop from one figure to the other. Then he drew a straight dashed line between them. He turned around and said, 'Fans love to see the Bomb thrown this way,' pointing to the big loop. 'They ooh and ahh as the ball is soaring through the air and they watch the receiver. Now (pointing to the straight line) this is how I want the Bomb thrown. Get it to the receiver as quick as you can and don't let the other guys get it.' I'll never forget that meeting."

Charlie Ward is considered to be one of the finest quarterbacks in the history of college football. Winner of the 1993 Heisman Trophy, Ward led FSU to the national championship that same season and lost just two games as a starter his whole career. It didn't start off that way, however. Ward threw eight interceptions in the first two games of his junior season in 1992. The Seminoles defeated both Duke and Clemson, but lost 19-16 to Miami two games later. With a 5-1 record, FSU was on the road at Georgia Tech and it appeared the

Yellow Jackets had FSU beaten with the Seminole offense sputtering all day and trailing 21-7 in the fourth quarter. At that point, Bowden listened to his offensive assistants and his own gut and shifted Ward to the shotgun, spread out the Seminole receivers and proceeded to let "Charlie be Charlie" as he carved up the Tech defense in a come-from-behind win.

The "Fast Break" offense might not have been born at Florida State, but Bowden learned that day that he needed to adopt it to win with that team. So, he went "all in" on the offense that eventually brought him his first national title.

General Buster Hagenbeck is a recognized leader in his own right and the former Superintendent of the U.S. Military Academy. He cut his coaching teeth as a graduate assistant at Florida State and included Bowden's learning and listening skills as keys to his success. He told me over the phone: "I've observed three qualities that made Coach Bowden an outstanding leader:

1. His character. He was a genuine person and a leader of complete integrity.
2. His competence. He was a continuous leader and a great listener. He'd ask questions of experts and then implement their ideas.
3. His caring. He cared about the University, the football program and each one of his players. He was one of a kind."

IT'S NOT ME IT'S WE

Team building is one of the most critical challenges of any leader. It doesn't matter if you are in charge of the concession stand at your daughter's softball complex, the church bar-b-que or the launch of your company's new product line, you have got to be able to gather the strays in your group, get everyone lined up the same way and get them to pull together to form a team.

Bobby Bowden walked into the proverbial "herding cats" challenge when he took over at Florida State. We heard from one of the lone stars on that team, Mike Shumann, earlier. "When Bobby Bowden arrived we were really flailing as a program," he admitted. "We'd had an 0-11 season the year before and were headed nowhere. His message to us was, 'You are responsible to your teammates and the team.' Up until that point, we were all looking out for ourselves. We had no sense of unity at all. Coach got us started working together as a team to get better and we stopped fighting against each other. We even started doing anything for our teammates."

Coach Bowden, like many successful leaders, used a combination of a change in atmosphere and change in relationships to effect an overall change in production.

"Coach created a true family atmosphere at FSU," said Clay Shiver who was an All-American center on FSU's 1993 National Championship team and who had a brother, Stan, who was a standout safety for Bowden before that. "Creating that atmosphere was his focus and he instilled that in all of us. It started with the recruiting process when he'd invite you to join his FSU family. We had a tight bond with everyone and that's what made us so powerful."

The more people I interviewed about Bobby Bowden the more his unique relationship with the players emerged. He treated them with respect and that created loyalty, commitment, effort and teamwork. It will do the same for your team.

"Many mornings Coach would be coming through the front door and I would see him holding the door open for the custodian, or one of our swimmers," said FSU strength and conditioning coordinator Jon Jost. "And he wouldn't leave it at that. He always engaged them with a 'nice to see you, Buddy, or come on in, Gal.' He treated the players and coaches with equal respect."

Ronald Lewis was on the receiving end of one of the most important touchdowns in Florida State history. He caught a post pattern for a touchdown to defeat Nebraska in the 1987 Fiesta Bowl. He said, "Coach treated all of his players with respect. You could be a star or a reserve and it didn't matter to Coach Bowden. He dealt with all of us the same way, which made everyone feel comfortable."

Dr. David Castillo was an outstanding center for the Seminoles from 2002-05 and is now in the family medicine residency program. "Coach treated everyone with respect whether you were a lifelong friend or he just met you at a booster function," he said. "As a player, you felt like everyone was an equal part in the success that we achieved."

And it is clear that the respect was returned.

"Coach was so good at motivating people," said Lee Good who was a manager at West Virginia. "He had an air that commanded respect. He didn't have to demand it because we all knew that he cared about his athletes."

Dan Mowrey was the kicker on FSU's great early 1990s teams. "We all had the utmost respect for Coach," said Mowrey. "He was the E.F. Hutton of our generation. He didn't demand our respect but we just gave it to him. He just had a presence about him that made us want to do that."

"He respected our opinions as defensive coaches," said Jack Stanton, who coached for Bowden in the early years at FSU. "That first season in 1976 he questioned everything we did, but as he gained confidence in us, he left us alone. "

IT AIN'T BY ACCIDENT

Do you recall the story from earlier in the book about Bowden's meticulous note taking? I told you about the fact that he left my co-writer a box with every single note he wrote for each of the seasons he was at Florida State.

I talked Rob into popping one open at random. One note from practice read: "August 10, not getting effort out of #8. Team looks tired. Remind them they have to be able to think when exhausted." Another pulled out at random read, "special teams dragging to the line; remind them they are equal parts with offense and defense." Still another, this from 1993 read, "ask everyone to evaluate whether players appear entitled…remind team of big upsets…coachs' gear looks rag tag to me."

Many of those close to Bowden bristle at any suggestion that his practice of delegating important tasks to his assistants translated into a lack of involvement in the coaching of his team. It was clear that it was a perception that some rival coaches tried to spread on the recruiting trail, particularly late in his career.

"Good grief my own sons Tommy and Terry were about as bad about it as anyone when they were at Clemson and Auburn," Bowden said chuckling. "They used to say things like, 'Could Dad find his way to the door?' or 'You know he probably doesn't know what position you play.' They would be kidding, but they also kind of would be injecting that."

The fact that his hand was on the rudder of the ship was never in question among his players. John Davis played safety at FSU from 1989-92. He said, "Coach always had a plan. He made sure all the pieces were in place to execute his plan. He hated to lose and to me he was the ultimate warrior. He was always prepared for whatever we would face on game day. He knew what would happen in a game before it happened. It was amazing."

Dayne Williams scored 24 touchdowns from his fullback position from 1986-88 for Florida State. "Coach and his staff always had a good game plan ready for us," said Williams. "The man studied film, was very organized and always had us prepared for Saturday. During the game, if necessary, he was willing to adjust the game plan quickly. At the end of the day, Coach Bowden took ownership of the program and didn't point fingers. He was an incredible coach and it was a privilege to play for him."

"We were always well prepared by Coach and his staff," agreed Theon Rackley in a quote that almost reads verbatim to Williams' although Theon played linebacker ten years later than Williams. "We never took any opponent lightly. Coach made every team sound like they were 10-0. The man worked hard and that made us want to follow. He gave us all the tools to be winners, made sure we were ready and after that it was up to us."

Jarad Moon played center for the Seminoles and eventually married the daughter of FSU assistant coach Chuck Amato. He said, "Coach Bowden set a standard that was nearly impossible to achieve. He demanded excellence and 100 guys would run through a wall because he cared about us. At the same time, he demanded that we run through that wall. It was a balance of the grandfatherly style and the hard-driving, demanding head football coach. The bottom line on Bobby Bowden as a leader is that he cared about people, but demanded excellence. You want to play for a man like that."

FSU placekicker Richie Andrews remembers the famous *Puntrooskie*, which we illustrate in detail in Chapter 6. "Coach put hours of preparation into each week leading up to game day," he recounted. "We practiced that Puntrooskie all week. There was a real buzz on the sideline because we knew it was going to work. We called Coach "the riverboat gambler" because he knew when to roll the dice. He knew what he was talking about which gave us a lot of confidence in him."

Steve Gabbard played defensive tackle for the Seminoles from 1985-88 and went on to play six years in the NFL before serving as a graduate assistant to Bowden at FSU. He suggests Bowden's organization was not appreciated by many. "Some people are surprised when I tell them Coach Bowden was the most organized person I've ever known," Gabbard said. "Every minute of his day was planned to the last detail. Every practice was broken down into five minute blocks. I guess the media focused on his personality and wide open style so they missed that."

Steve Gilmer played in the secondary for Bowden at FSU from 1991-94.

"Coach really believed that details matter," he was quick to tell me. "Doing the little things well ended up making the difference in success and failure. For example, running to and from drills or doing them the right way or we do it again. That has carried over into my business as well. A simple thing like returning phone calls can end up making the difference in how successful your business is going to be."

"He had an uncanny ability to handle details," said former Florida State linebacker Willie Pauldo. "He knew everything about the team even when you thought he didn't. He'd be up in that tower taking in everything. Later on he'd come up to you and tell you what he spotted and tell you what to do."

An All-American in the classroom and on the field, Chris Hope was the free safety on FSU's 1999 national championship team and has been in the NFL since he was drafted by the Steelers in 2002. "Coach was a little older when I played for him and the man was still all-seeing," said Hope. "He'd make notes on the smallest details at practice. I've learned that it was stuff that was not big enough to win a game, but small enough to lose a game."

Mark Salva played on Bowden's FSU offensive line and then got a peak behind the curtain as a graduate assistant under him. "Coach was a stickler for details," said Salva who went on to become a full-time assistant at South Carolina. "He insisted that every high school in Florida be visited by an FSU coach every year. He didn't want to go to a high school clinic and have a coach tell him, 'We never see any of your coaches.'"

And Joe Ostazewski had a similar experience having played defensive line for the Seminoles and then returning to coach. "Coach was an amazing delegator," he said. "His preparation and planning were precise. He never missed a thing. He included all of his staff and utilized their skills to the maximum. He'd give us our assignments and then held us accountable."

West Virginia's team captain from 1970 agrees. "Coach was very dedicated to his profession and expected a lot of himself and that never changed," said John Hale. "He was a stickler for preparation and hard work. He wanted flawless execution of those tasks he set in front of us. He set a high personal example for us in the work department."

YOU BETTER BE FLEXIBLE

Few leaders have a career that spanned 58 years, but Bobby Bowden did. You want an expert on dealing with change? Look no further.

When Bobby Bowden took over the FSU program in 1976, length of hair was one of the first questions lobbed at the man in his first press conference. His answer was priceless: "Folks, if length of hair had anything to do with winning ball games, Army and Navy would still be playing for the national championship every year."

Bowden's coaching legacy spanned the era of "yes sir, no sir," "you can't drink water during practice" to dealing with drugs and single parent families to today's smorgasbord of tattoos, unchecked cursing and society's celebration of disrespect.

"I remember one day Coach called me and asked me if I had any clip-on earrings," said Sue Hall. "I told him I did and brought them in. Next thing I know he's headed for a team meeting wearing the earrings. He could get his point across when he wanted to."

Gary Huff is one of the finest quarterbacks in the history of Florida State and played and coached in the NFL. He marveled at Bowden's ability to change.

"Just think about the span of time when Bobby Bowden was coaching," he said. "This stands out in my mind. You always had a hard and fast rule in early football. You would teach a punt returner to never, ever take a step back once he caught the ball. It wasn't even a question. Now, did Bobby Bowden tell Deion Sanders not to take a step back? Heck no! He recognized greatness and he had the competence and flexibility to change with that. A lot of coaches would have still been trying to tell Deion to take a knee."

EVERYBODY TILTS, THE GOOD ONES REALIGN

Balance between his professional life and his personal life emerged as one of Bear Bryant's greatest weaknesses during my research for *Bear Bryant on Leadership*. I find that to be true of a number of leaders. It makes sense given how easy it is for them to get tunnel vision in their drive to succeed. We all leave families sitting at home wondering when we'll walk through the door. Bowden had to do that as well, but his ability to balance his life emerges as perhaps his greatest strength.

"Football is not my god," Bobby Bowden proclaimed to the astonishment of many when his FSU program was emerging on the national scene. "For me it is my faith first, family second and football third. I believe you have got to have your priorities right. Now, it doesn't matter if you coach football like I do or clean up the stadium after the game. You have got to have your priorities straight."

"Coach was very close to his family," said Sue Hall. "They meant so much to him and still do. He'd have a Bible reading every morning with the children and still does with Ann. Bobby's children idolized him. When Ann walks into a room, his face still just lights up. He is still very much in love with her."

Rich Duggan saw it at West Virginia in 1975. "Coach was defined by his actions off the field," he said. "His life was defined by his faith and his family. Those were his most important life values, not just football."

"Coach had a strong work ethic, but he understood the importance of balance" said FSU team chaplain Clint Purvis. "He kept his family intact, took care of his health and kept in close touch with the Lord at all times."

Drew Weatherford was the Seminole starting quarterback in 2006 and 2007.

"His faith served as the foundation of his life," he said. "He was unshakable in tough situations because his faith gave him a resolve second to none. His life was not a yoyo experience going up with the good days and down with the bad. Coach would take our defeats and use them to get better as a team and as individuals. These were great lessons that helped us succeed in the end."

Jimbo Fisher succeeded his mentor as head coach of the Seminoles in 2010 and had the benefit of coaching under him for three years before taking the job. "Coach never got too high or too low," said Fisher who has returned FSU to the preseason Top 10 in 2011. "I'm sure that came from the experience gained is so many years of coaching, but it kept his staff in a nice balanced frame of mind."

Florida State star linebacker Kendyll Pope knew Bowden's motivations.

"His family always came first and that carried over to the FSU football program which helped the school become such a great power for years," said Pope who played for FSU from 2000-2003 before playing for the Indianapolis Colts. "When the great talent arrived in Tallahassee, Coach treated everyone equally. We all got the same opportunity to play and show what we could do. That is why the man was loved so much. So many of his players came from fatherless homes and Coach filled that void. He taught us that school was important and so was church. He wanted us to grow up and become successful adults. When Coach Bowden finished his coaching career, his former players all felt as if we'd lost our father."

I admire John Wooden and read every word I can about him. He said that the two most important words in the English language were "love" and "balance."

While Bobby Bowden would be quick to point out how Ann basically had to raise the children, the overwhelming evidence shows that his ability to keep everything in his life in the right priority sets him apart from even his most accomplished leadership peers.

SMILING NEVER HURT ANYBODY

When Rob Wilson and I talked on the phone about the idea of this book, I followed our conversation with an email of my Seven Dimensions of Leadership. I got an email back first thing the next morning from Rob saying the illustration for *charisma* is "done." "Done," I thought, "We haven't even really decided to work together."

I would see why just a few short weeks later when he told me about the trip to Las Vegas and the ESPY's you read about earlier.

Remember that Bowden was invited to the 2000 ESPY's in Vegas along with a boat load of both sports and entertainment celebrities. The event was huge even in Vegas terms. The celebrities from both worlds stayed in the MGM Grand and were taken by limo from the back door around to the banquet hall in the same hotel, for Pete's sake.

ESPN had all the celebrities report to holding rooms 90 minutes before the program – one for the sports world and one for entertainment celebrities. So literally elbow to elbow were Pete Sampras, Justin Leonard, Annika Sorenstam, Mario Lemieux and many, many more in the sports room.

It would be a few minutes later that Bowden's charisma would astound even a longtime associate like Rob. Bowden does not drink and has never been fond of cocktail parties. He's never been comfortable making small talk in that kind of environment, so Wilson was not surprised when Bowden headed for a table in the corner by himself, clearly with no intention of moving until the awards show began. Wilson told me that maybe 15 minutes later everyone heard gales of laughter from a table in the corner. He looked over and seated around Bowden were Burt Reynolds, James Caan (both of whom had snuck over from the other room) along with Dick Vermeil and standing over them straining to join in the fun were NFL legends Reggie White and Jerry Rice. No sooner had the laughter died down than actor Michael Clark Duncan, whose movie *The Green Mile* had just been released, came in the room and spotted Bowden. He rushed over with his arms open wide and said, "Bobby Bowden you are one of my favorite coaches." Bowden looked up without missing a beat and said, "I saw your picture (he always calls movies pictures) last night and I loved it." Duncan stopped in his tracks with a huge smile on his face.

Folks, that's charisma.

Kamerion Wimbley is starring in the NFL, but before that he played defensive end for Bowden at Florida State. "Coach was such a charismatic guy and had an aura about him," he said. "People wanted to be around him. His coaching history was part of that. He had a great track record, so his players were thinking, 'This man knows what he is doing and he's worthy of following.' Coach Bowden instilled so much in my life: family values, business principles, my NFL career and above all how to be a man."

Even his own son could see it. "Dad had great charisma and communication skills and that helped to elevate all of his people who were working with him," said former Auburn and current North Alabama head coach Terry Bowden. "He never got caught up with fame or recognition. He could make fun of himself by using self-deprecating humor. That made him approachable and very much like a real down-to-earth person."

Former NFL executive Ernie Accorsi saw it early in Bowden's Florida State days. He told me, "I went to Florida State one spring for their pro day. All the NFL guys were sitting in a room waiting for Bobby Bowden to appear. When he walked in, I was impressed with how friendly Bowden was and how all the pro guys reacted to him."

Bob Zitelli said things hadn't changed much since he played offensive guard at West Virginia from 1967-72. "I had trust and confidence in Coach and was always willing to go the second mile for him," he said. "To this day, he's like a magnet with his players. Whenever we see him, we still flock to him. "

Josh Robbins writes for the *Orlando Sentinel* and covered the Seminole beat for a time during the Bowden era. "Bobby Bowden possessed one trait that few of his contemporaries in college coaching had and that was charm," Robbins said. "Employing a home-spun, self-deprecating sense of humor, Bowden could captivate an individual or an entire group. It is one reason why he was considered college football's ultimate closer on the recruiting circuit."

"Coach Bowden had more charisma than any coach ever," proclaimed Ken Braswell who played defensive end and linebacker at West Virginia from 1975-78. "I cried when he left. He got the best out of every one of his players. He could grab a hold of anybody."

Kirk Carruthers was one of the players that Bowden traveled a long way to recruit. He was from East Lansing, Michigan and his dad had been an assistant with then Michigan State head coach George Perles. In fact, Perles was best man at his parent's wedding. "The first time I met Coach Bowden he became an instant father-figure," said Carruthers who would go on to star at linebacker for the Seminoles from 1988-91. "I felt his charisma and developed an instant attraction to him. From that first meeting, I wanted him to be a mentor in my life. He just had this special gift of leading by example. He was always walking the walk and only special leaders have that gift."

Tallahassean David Palmer is now a practicing physician but before that he played linebacker for Bobby Bowden on FSU teams from 1984-87. "I think all great leaders have charisma," said Dr. Palmer. "I use the phrase *positive energy* and you feel it when you are around Coach Bowden. I spoke to him recently at age 81 and he still has that quality. That's what attracted me to him almost 30 years ago."

In the locker room following the 1993 Orange Bowl in which Florida State beat Nebraska 18-16 for the national championship, Bowden was told that President Clinton was on the phone. He didn't freeze up. "Hey buddy, why aren't you working tonight?" was how he opened the conversation.

I could fill another book on Bowden's poise, his appreciation and respect for history, and his perspective and judgment all of which are fundamental elements in a competent leader, but we're running out of room. However, I can't leave this chapter on competence without reflecting on one of his most pronounced strengths.

DON'T BE SOMETHING YOU'RE NOT

Flip back to Chapter Four on character and tell me how someone can be honest, responsible and possess integrity and not be themselves? I contend that it can't be done. One cannot be a successful leader at any level by "acting" out the role.

It seems simple enough but just consider all the distracting forces pulling on a major leader. In a football coach's case he's got alumni demanding he be this way, mothers demanding he be another way, starters wanting him to act this way and bench warmers hoping he is another. A corporate leader faces the same desire to please share holders, his rank and file workers, the consumers and the media. A lot of different people are pulling on the coattails of the leader.

A leader better be himself or run the risk of the same fate that awaits a lie. Tell a lie often enough and it becomes the truth. Act rather than lead and eventually you will lose sight of who you are.

John Swofford is the Commissioner of the Atlantic Coast Conference and a person who worked closely with Bowden over the years. He explained: "He was consistent and genuine, and therefore evoked trust from those he was leading. He had great empathy for those around him, whether players, coaches, media or fans. He was tremendously loyal to his players. He was bold, as evidenced by his willingness in his early years of building the FSU program to play anybody, anywhere. He was value driven. His faith and his principles guided his leadership and behavior. What an example to follow in how you conduct yourself and how you should treat people. What an influence he has been when you see someone be so successful, yet never try to be anyone but himself. Bobby is so genuine. He always handled himself with such class, dignity and humility, whether he was winning, which was most of the time, or after a loss or when he was being unfairly criticized, as coaches so often are. He was always so positive. Just watching him has been truly inspiring to me. No matter what your age, he is such a great example of how to live your life, and he has done that under great scrutiny in a very public role over a long period of time. That's hard to do!"

"Bobby Bowden didn't live on praise and wasn't destroyed by criticism," said former Florida State Athletic Director Bob Goin. "Bobby knew his place on this earth and was trying to please God and do his will. He wanted to win football games, but never got too high or too low. His engine didn't run on others' evaluation of him. Because of his faith in God, Coach was very comfortable in his own skin."

We heard from Steve Gabbard earlier and he also talked about Bowden's sincerity. He said, "He's the most famous person who is the real deal you'll ever meet. Coach is the genuine article and when he says he's a Christian he is. When he says he's a self-disciplined man, he is as well. Coach always lived the life he asked of his players and very few do that. Players have an intuition when it comes to reading coaches. We seem to be equipped with the radar to do that. That's why Coach did so well as a recruiter. Players and their families knew he was the genuine article before they even got to know him."

More and more the modern profile of a "great leader" in today's society seems to be a rigid character who exudes strength. It is almost as if showing a sense of humor somehow diminishes their strength. Bowden never suffered from trying to put on that front.

Vickie Roberts started 32 straight games at offensive guard at West Virginia from 1967-70, and appreciated Bowden's personality. "I watch coaches today and they always seem to have a scowl on their face and appear to be so unhappy," he said. "Coach Bowden never lost his ability to laugh. He'd use that southern charm to his advantage, too. He was serious when it came to football, but he never forgot the importance of laughter every day.

"I went down to his last game at the Gator Bowl. I told him later about how emotional the FSU fans were. I said, 'Coach, there are a lot of good looking women crying because you're leaving' and he turned to me and asked, 'Did you get any names and phone numbers?' "

"Dad made people feel good about working with him, every one of them," said Terry Bowden. "They all had a good experience and enjoyed their time with him. He had the ability to make people feel good about themselves. Every player and coach felt their time with Dad was extremely worthwhile."

One more story from my co-writer and it revolves around the mundane grind of ACC football media day. Every conference has one where they fly all the coaches in to meet with tons of media spread out all over a hotel convention center. Coaches have to trudge from one room to another answering the same questions over and over again. It drives some coach's crazy, but Bowden never looked at it that way.

"We were outside Atlanta one year doing the gauntlet of TV and radio interviews when Coach told me a joke during the short delay between rooms," Wilson said. "I didn't laugh very hard and he realized I had already heard the joke and the challenge was on. We would try and tell each other a joke that the other one had not heard between every interview. I'd get maybe 20 words into a joke and he'd put his hand up, 'Heard it,' he'd snap. Then I would do the same. The stereotypical thing for him to do would have been to join his peers in looking at their watches and letting out exasperated sighs, but not Coach Bowden."

I was even told by one person who wanted to remain anonymous that Bowden wouldn't step out of character even when it would help his own cause.

"We had a rival coach that was accusing us of some things and it got pretty nasty," the administrator would tell me. "We compiled a tape that showed that coach's team doing the very things he was accusing us of. We went in to try and get Coach to lash back in the media. He just put his foot down and said, 'You know, that's just not me. They'll get theirs.' And that was it."

How do you sum up Bobby Bowden's competence as a leader? I'll let Ben Odom do that for us. He was a walk-on, reserve, quarterback for the Seminoles after leading his high school team in Lake City, Florida, to the state championship. He went on to earn his law degree while serving as a graduate assistant under Bowden at Florida State. "Coach always seemed to know what to say and do," said Odom. "A situation would present itself and he would say, 'Have you considered this, have you considered that?' He was just brilliant the way he handled any situation. As a world leader he could have solved world problems. It's a shame he was only a football coach."

Chapter Six:

WAS THAT A LITTLE MUCH?

"Of course, I've been in many games where I knew we could lose it, but I NEVER went into a game not trying to win it. I've gone into a game where my thinking is, 'We don't have a chance, but I'm going to do everything I can to beat him.' "

—BOBBY BOWDEN

reat leaders must be bold and they must make decisions. Coaches and players from Howard, to South Georgia, to West Virginia and finally Florida State have filled this book with stories and memories of Bobby Bowden and underlying nearly every one is an admiration for the boldness that he showed as a coach and a leader.

Bobby Bowden didn't have the advantage of taking over programs that were "can't miss" opportunities. He showed boldness in just believing that taking over at South Georgia College would be the route to eventual major college success. Imagine the courage he summoned in taking over at FSU when even the most dedicated of fans were beginning to believe there was no hope for success.

Mike Sherwood quarterbacked West Virginia from 1968-70. He said, "Coach Bowden was very strong in his own convictions. He'd make decisions and then live with the outcome without being influenced by what others thought. He'd do what he thought was right, then stick with it."

"When Coach started with us at West Virginia, he was coaching during traumatic times in society and he had his hands full," said Mountaineer tight end Randy Flinchum. "But he was a fiery little son of a gun and was up to the task."

We all got a clear example of a great leader's boldness and courage when Florida State played Clemson on national television in 1988. Replays of the famous Puntrooskie serve as a fantastic lesson in boldness, courage and leadership.

THE PUNTROOSKIE

Florida State was loaded in 1988 with Deion Sanders, Sammie Smith, Odell Haggins and some 11 other future NFL players. For the first time ever, FSU was ranked No. 1 going into the season. The players talked Bowden into letting them record a rap video, which blew up in their faces when Miami crushed the Seminoles 31-0 in the season-opener in the Orange Bowl. Two weeks later, FSU found itself in an absolute dog-fight with Danny Ford's Clemson Tigers.

The home-standing Tigers had pushed an ineffective Florida State offense around all day and appeared ready to salt the game away. Clemson had tied the game at 21 with just over two minutes left and then pinned FSU back at its own 21-yard line where FSU faced fourth and long.

Step back a moment here and consider the decision facing Bowden. A second loss this early in the season would crush what had been billed as potentially Florida State's greatest season ever. He was facing a fourth down play that needed to gain four yards with an offense that had struggled all day. Nothing seemed to be working. The momentum had completely shifted to Clemson and the Death Valley crowd was frenzied. A great punt would still give them good field position with all the momentum in the world and needing only a field goal.

What do you do?

Well, if we've learned nothing else in this book we have learned that Bowden is the consummate leader, and having those qualities means you have had the competence to have worked out a plan in practice that you might employ here. It means you've evaluated your team's talents so you know who to call on; you have delegated the responsibility of having your special teams ready; you have inspired optimism and hope in all those you lead; and now you will call on your personal courage, boldness and decisiveness and make a decision.

All week long Florida State had worked on a trick play called the Puntrooskie. Bowden had learned the play from a graduate assistant named Clint Ledbetter who had used it as a player at Arkansas State. The Puntrooskie, naturally, was called in a punting situation. The center would snap the ball to the blocking back – not the punter – while the punter would fake like the snap had soared over his head. As the defenders would chase up field, the back would slip the ball between the legs of one of the lineman, freshman defensive back LeRoy Butler.

Butler would then have to hesitate for a moment before shooting off to his left and hopefully scamper down field for a score.

FSU had practiced it so often during the week that the players admitted they were sure the coaches would call it against Clemson. However, during the course of the game Florida State lined up several times to punt and assistants and players looked at Bowden for him to pull the trigger, but either momentum or field position caused him to wave it off.

Now, back to the dire situation with the game on the line. If Bowden called the trick play on the 21-yard line and it failed he surely would give Clemson the win. It was a huge gamble, but Bowden sent in the play. Butler, who would go on to a Hall of Fame career as a safety at FSU and 12 years with the Green Bay Packers, even asked Bowden if he was 'sure he wanted to call that play.'

FSU lined up and pulled off the play without a hitch as Butler raced down the Clemson team sideline all the way to the 1-yard line as a complete hush fell over the stadium. It was pandemonium on the Florida State sideline as well as the ABC broadcast booth where Brent Musburger described the stunning turn of events to the nation.

On Sunday after the Seminoles kicked the field goal and won, Beano Cook called it "the greatest play since 'My Fair Lady',"" and he didn't get any arguments.

Just think what would have happened if that play hadn't worked. Florida State would have tried some "silly" fluke play that was too complicated to possibly work and one of those big old Clemson defensive linemen would have squashed Butler like a bug in the middle of that pileup. The Tigers would have run three dive plays, lined up for the gimme field goal and trotted on out of the stadium with a win. Instead of Bowden making all the media members get up so he could use their press room chairs to reenact all the moving parts in the play, he would have had to justify his "bone-headed" call.

It was an educated gamble on the part of one of the finest coaches college football has ever known, but it wasn't the "pull a play out of a hat" type of call that many seemed to suggest. They had prepared for the moment, he had conditioned his team, and he had the boldness to make the call.

Wow!

It doesn't always work. A Bowden trick play at Auburn one year blew up in his face. *Coke* launched *New Coke*. Somehow a car called the AMC Pacer was allowed to actually hit the streets. Leaders certainly aren't insulated from bold decisions.

Phil Carrollo walked on to the FSU team and played from 1986-88. He said, "Coach taught us to weigh the risk component and if you do that it's not as big as people think. Coach was never afraid to open a game with a risky play, but we were always prepared. Therefore, it was not just a roll of the dice, but a calculated risk. I've taken that approach strategy into my business."

Rocky Gianola played center at West Virginia from 1974-78. "You could tell right away that he would have a tremendous career," he said. "He has such an innovative offensive approach that brought out our confidence because he exuded such confidence."

Zeke Zakowsky played defensive end at West Virginia from 1971-74 and said he appreciated Bowden's style. "He was like a general out front leading you," he said. "Coach would always do whatever he asked his players to do. He was a hands on communicator."

And Terry Voithofer, who was a captain of the Mountaineers in 1971, suggests the bottom line for Bowden was trust. "He led by example and never let us down," he said.

DECISIVENESS IS IMPORTANT!

Have you ever stopped to think how critical being decisive is to leadership? Imagine how uninspiring Harry Truman would have appeared had his quote been, "Well, I, uhhh, suppose that I might be the one, where you could, maybe, lay down the buck."

Bobby Bowden never had any problem being indecisive. He admits that a lot of that came from his faith and fundamental beliefs. Others saw and appreciated this quality in him.

"Coach was a very decisive leader," said FSU linebacker Ed Clark who played from 1989-92. "He made difficult decisions with apparent ease. I remember one incident when I was at FSU. We had a player who was murdered, so it was a traumatic time for all of us. Coach had to handle the team and the media. I remember how decisive he was. He decided what to do and then did it. We didn't see him second-guess himself. Coach had faith in his God which gave him confidence. He was going in the right direction. It's easy to follow a leader like that."

Back in the late 1960s, Bowden was drilling decisiveness into his players at West Virginia. "One of my favorite Bobby Bowden quotes was, 'Do something, even if is wrong, and go with reckless abandon,'" said defensive end John Hale. "That quote has stuck with me for over 40 years."

Theodore Roosevelt once said, "The unforgivable crime is soft hitting. Do not hit at all if it can be avoided; but never hit softly." I think Teddy Roosevelt and Bobby Bowden would have gotten along quite nicely.

West Virginia tight end Bubba Coker remembers Bobby Bowden as a perfectionist. "When I close my eyes today and think of Bobby Bowden, he's standing on the sideline sending in a play," said Coker. "I hear him say, 'Dadgum it...run it right!' He wanted every play to be perfect."

Fred McMillan played linebacker at West Virginia from 1968-73 and he said they recognized early on that Bowden was special. "Way back in our day, we knew he was an offensive genius and way ahead of the game," he told me. "As a leader, he was very fair to his players and a man everybody liked. Coach Bowden was the greatest person I've been associated with in my lifetime."

Bobby Bowden had to handle some really difficult situations over his career. He used humor to deflect some of the tension, but he also was decisive in his answers. For a while, the media chased him around like a group of dogs after a raccoon asking him about the glaring missing jewel from his crown – the lack of a national championship.

Bowden turned the tables on them in 1993 just a few days before playing Nebraska in the Orange Bowl in a game that either Tom Osborne or Bobby Bowden would win for their first title. Naturally, they were both getting questions about how they would feel if they were the one who missed a chance in a few nights.

"Let me ask all y'all something," Bowden said in the press hotel. "What is the highest honor in y'all's profession?" Someone offered the Pulitzer Prize. "How many of you have every won one of those awards?" he asked.

"Well, is the fact that you've never won driving you crazy?" Bowden continued. "Does the fact that you've never won mean you're no good at your profession? Are y'all failures? Are you obsessed with winning one of those awards? I'll bet you don't give a darn whether you ever win one of them or not. Now, if you win one, good. But I'll bet it ain't driving you crazy. That's about the way it always was with me about winning a national championship. It was not driving me crazy."

My co-writer was in that press conference with Bowden and still chuckles at the occasion. "It was just remarkable the clarity he gave to everyone in the room on that issue," Rob Wilson told me. "Even those of us closest to him realized why he felt like he did and the look on the writer's faces was like a veil had just been pulled off. I kind of chuckle because I know for a fact that there was indeed a Pulitzer Prize winner in the room, but I don't want to kill a great story either."

W.B. Newton was a linebacker at West Virginia before serving as one of Bowden's graduate assistant coaches. "I was up in the press box once I got to be a graduate assistant and I can assure you that Bobby Bowden had no trouble making a decision," he said.

Brent Kallestad covered much of Bobby Bowden's Florida State career for the *Associated Press* from the Tallahassee bureau. "Bowden never differentiated in his dealings with people whether they were so-called stars of network television, college newspaper reporters or big boosters," he said. "His humor often deflected potentially uncomfortable situations. On a couple of occasions I had to knock on the front door of his home to reach him (including the night he was being bumped out as coach) and was always graciously received by him and Ann. I think Bobby's innate decency may have been his most admirable quality."

It may seem strange to include that observation in the chapter on boldness, but dealing with the throng of media that a head coach faces daily takes that quality. It's nice that Bobby left the guy writing the AP stories with those kinds of memories.

"A day before the 1993 national championship game after a Florida State practice at the Orange Bowl, a couple of hundred fans waited for Bowden to finish his media interviews and encircled the media and coach," remembers Kallestad. "The morning had begun as a cool, overcast day and Bowden (already 64) was wearing a Florida State sweatshirt and by noon the clouds had disappeared and a hot South Florida sun was beating down. The day had become very muggy. Bobby (sweat pouring off of him) patiently waded through scores of media questions and then started signing autographs, asking people if they had a message or Bible verse they'd like to have him write in addition to his name. One Miami sports writer, Steve Wine, had one question he wasn't able to get in during the earlier gaggle and was waiting for Coach to finish up. Wine couldn't believe Bobby's patience, sincerity and good humor. I'll never forget what Steve said that day, "Boy, he loves people, doesn't he?"

"During a 9 a.m. New Year's Day practice in preparation for the 1999 national championship game in the Sugar Bowl against Michael Vick and Virginia Tech, only a few reporters showed up for the early workout and there wasn't much to talk about at that point with the game only a couple of days away," said Kallestad. "His star kicker, Sebastian Janikowski, was a noted rounder in Tallahassee and I just asked him somewhat teasingly if Sebastian made curfew the night before (New Years' Eve). Bobby, of course, couldn't lie. 'No, he was late.' It created a furor, a story in a week where there had been no controversy. Sebastian ran the steps for his misdeed, but Bowden was criticized for not disciplining him more severely. The sports information staff was upset with me for asking the question, saying, 'Brent, you know Bobby can't lie.' I didn't have a clue Janikowski had been out late and neither would have anyone else, but Bowden was honest."

And bold!

TWO MUST HAVES

Any study of leadership suggests that the successful leader has an abundance of courage and confidence. John Eason, FSU's receivers coach during the dynasty years, said Coach Bowden set the tone early.

"Before the start of fall practice, we would go on staff retreats," said Eason. "Coach would set the priorities for the season and we would go over in great detail how we would handle situations that were going to come up. He set the agenda for the year and all of his assistants knew very clearly that he was in charge."

Martin Mayhew, who grew up playing at Florida High School which was literally in the shadows of Doak Campbell Stadium, played cornerback for the Seminoles from 1984-87 and seven years in the NFL. He is now General Manager of the Detroit Lions. "Out on the football field it was undeniable who was in charge," Mayhew said. "Coach didn't need to raise his voice because it was apparent to all of us he was the top man. At practice he'd kneel down and watch carefully. He had a pad and he'd be writing things down constantly, about what we were doing that needed to be improved. You could bet he'd get those mistakes corrected quickly."

Lonnie Johnson played tight end in the NFL for five years retiring in 1999, but he and Bowden tussled during one point in his Seminole career. "I made a decision not to play as a junior," said Johnson. "I thought it would be best for my career to sit out and redshirt. Coach didn't agree and we had our moments over that one. Finally, he convinced me that my leadership was needed on the field. Ultimately, he made the decision and I played my senior season."

"Coach Bowden had the ability to make tough decisions," said Danny Kanell who threw 57 touchdown passes as FSU's quarterback from 1992-95. "That famous game with UF was a perfect example. We were down 31-3 and then started the comeback. It was 31-10, 31-24 and then we closed to 31-30. I was with Mark Richt (FSU's offensive coordinator) and he was thinking about going for two. Suddenly, we saw the kicker running onto the field and Coach holding one finger in the air. The kick was good and the game ended 31-31. We called it a great FSU win even though it was a tie. Later Coach said after such a great comeback, he couldn't risk a loss that would've ruined the day."

Bowden showed the same courage in going for a win against Miami in a battle of No. 3 vs. No. 4 in 1987. With :47 left on the clock and trailing 26-25, Bowden sent in rock-solid place kicker Derek Schmidt for the extra point that would leave the game in a tie. Earlier in the week, Bowden had explained to CBS' Brent Musburger that his team had lost to Miami in 1980, ruining the chance for a national championship because he had gone for two points and failed. But following a time out, Bowden went against those earlier comments and sent quarterback Danny McManus back in to try and win the game. The pass never reached the receiver and FSU lost 26-25.

Even rival quarterbacks had respect for Bobby Bowden. Chris Leak quarterbacked the Florida Gators to a national championship and admitted he played extra hard in the games against FSU, but not for the reason you might assume. Leak was recruited by Bowden and actually had the Seminoles down to one of his last five choices.

"His faith was a huge part of his leadership package," Leak told me. "His players loved playing for him. He was a man of great character and integrity as well as being an outstanding coach who took risks and was not afraid to make tough decisions."

One of the first quotes that I came across when researching the book just jumped off the page to me. Rob Wilson sent it my way and it was from a meeting Bowden had with ESPN announcers before a Florida State game. As you probably know, the announcers meet with the head coaches and key players in the days just before the game in hopes of getting a feel for what to expect. Some coaches are remarkably forthcoming during these times and some are tight-lipped. Bowden, I'm told, probably fell in the middle on that. He trusted the announcers but was always concerned that down the line would be somebody that might not be as trustworthy.

At any rate, Bowden was asked a question by a veteran color man. "Coach, what are you looking for in your quarterback?" he asked. The implied response was clearly whether he wanted him to look to throw before he runs, not turn the ball over, get the right play called, or any pat answers from which coaches draw. Bowden didn't miss a beat in an incredibly revealing response: "I'm looking for my quarterback to do what I expect him to do."

What a tremendous example of courage and confidence. In other words, I have confidence in myself and my staff and I want someone on that field who is going to play the way we want the game to go. Can't you just put yourself right on that sideline with Bowden's arm draped around your shoulders, 80,000 fans going crazy and Coach looking right into your eyes and telling you, "Son, just run what we call and read your keys and we'll be just fine."

PROPER DISCIPLINE TAKES BEING BOLD

A quick read of the title is going to send the reader down the wrong course. I bet you automatically assumed this would be all about tough love, unbending rules and ruling with an iron fist. It is, but only in some cases.

Some of the most critical stories written about Bobby Bowden during his FSU career take shots at his discipline policy. Many seemed determined to paint Bowden into a corner by suggesting his second chance policy was a convenient way to avoid punishing star players. The columns I read on this topic are really one-sided.

I was surprised to learn that Bobby Bowden had dismissed so many high-profile players from his football team. I was even more startled once I learned some of the facts. He certainly didn't seem to get much credit, particularly from media in this state, for dismissing the likes of Randy Moss and Laveranues Coles, a couple of future NFL All-Pros.

Bowden showed tremendous courage in sticking to his discipline policy. "It would have been so much easier at times to just kick guys off the team with no regard for whether that was right or not," he said. "The media would have said, 'Way to go FSU' for about a day and then the kid would have to live with that the rest of his life. I told people, I'm never going to let the public, the fans and especially the media tell me what to do when it comes to disciplining my players. They have no standing and a lot of times they don't know whether the story they are printing is even correct or not. I was not going to sacrifice a boy for the sake of satisfying the dadgum press or the public."

I have talked to hundreds of his former players and while a majority of them suggested how tough Bowden was, I didn't find a single one who suggested he ever looked the other way on anything. Bowden himself saw a change in the way he viewed discipline and wrote about it with his son Steve in the outstanding first-person book *The Bowden Way.*

"I started out my career as a strident disciplinarian," Bowden said in the collection of his own leadership observations. "It was short hair, "yes, sir" and "no, sir," no tattoos, no earrings, and absolutely no disrespect toward the coaches. Definitely my way or the highway. Any player who challenged my rules was dismissed from the team. And any coach who divorced or drank alcoholic beverages or used drugs could not be kept on staff. I was a child of my times who also happened to have a strong religious upbringing. Many of my expectations, especially regarding player discipline, were typical of that era.

"As I passed through my 40s, 50s and 60s, and now during my 70s, I have eased up somewhat, except in regard to morality and my personal ideals. Someone once said if you hold a bird in your hand too tightly, you will kill it, but if you hold too loosely, it will get away. I squeezed a little too tightly in my younger years."

You would need Novocain and pliers to pull an admission of that sort out of most top leaders today. They couldn't possibly be caught admitting that they've changed with the times.

"The biggest disciplinary mistake I've made during my career, and I've made it more than once, is waiting too long before kicking a player off my team," admitted Bowden in *The Bowden Way*. "My reluctance had nothing to do with winning games. I just hate to give up on a kid if there's some way to help improve his life.

"I'm not thinking here of the player who commits a major crime or fails a drug test or physically abuses his girlfriend. Those boys are automatically dismissed. I'm thinking, rather, of the 1,001 problems you have with any boy between the ages of 18 and 22."

His players never saw Bowden as "easy" when it came to discipline.

"I was 20 years old and was the first causality of the Bowden era," admitted Bernie Kirchner a wide receiver at West Virginia from 1970-74. "After the Peach Bowl, he told us he'd kick us off the team if we violated team rules. I got caught drinking and was off the squad for the entire 1973 season. I played baseball and came back to football in '74. I wasn't happy with the whole experience, but it helped me mature as a man. I respect Bobby Bowden to this day."

We've heard from Clay Shiver several times in the book and he had the honor of serving as a team captain on FSU's 1993 national championship team. "Once I became captain, I would be called to Coach's office when we had a player in trouble over a team infraction," said Shiver. "Coach would ask me, 'What do you think I should do? If

I keep this player, will he be a cancer on the squad?' Coach was seeking a balance. The rules were the rules, but he wanted to be fair and treat each person individually because they were all different. For example, he would say to me; 'You have no excuse to miss class because I know your parents.' He wouldn't give me any leeway, but with other players he would."

"Coach was firm, but very fair," said Randy Flinched who played tight end from 1967-70 at W.V.U. "I got out of line with my behavior a few times, but Coach would give me a second chance and I am still grateful he did. I went on to coach high school football for 28 years and when a discipline issue came up I'd think, 'What would Coach do here?' The answer was, 'Don't rush to judgment.' I'd give kids a second chance and it never came back to haunt me."

Bobby Rhodes played for FSU at the same time his brother Billy did, and they both followed their dad who was a Seminole star. He said, "Coach was a great guy to be around. He was extremely nice to be with on and off the field. However, you never wanted to be on his bad side. If that happened, he'd be very strict with you."

The legendary Keith Jackson called many a Bobby Bowden coached game. "Bobby was a disciplinarian, he just had a different way of doing it," said Jackson in that voice that just sings football. "He was not a thunder and lightning guy. His physique would not bring fear, but his demeanor would. The way Bobby looked at you was quite disarming. All he needed with a big tackle who was causing trouble was about 30 seconds. Bobby would take the fire right out of him. Either that or there'd be a car waiting to remove the kid from campus."

"Coach got criticized for lack of discipline in his program, but most of it was unfair," said Florida State star safety from the late 1980s, Monk Bonasorte. "When I go out to speak to groups I would ask this question if it came up. 'How many of you parents would kick one of your children out of the house permanently if they violated one of your rules?' No hands would ever go up. Then I'd explain that these players were Bobby's kids. Many of them did not have fathers and were young men who needed help. Coach was willing to give them second chances to play football and receive a college degree. That second chance saved a lot of really good people."

One of those folks is Mike Shumann, who we heard from earlier in the book. He was one of the few stars when Bobby arrived at Florida State in 1976. Shumann was charged with a serious offense and Bowden sat him down for an entire season, but left a chance for him to return to the team. "I got a second chance and made the most of it," said Shumann. Indeed he did. He went on to play five years in the NFL, and is now one of the top sportscasters the San Francisco/Oakland market.

Danny Kanell succeeded Charlie Ward as quarterback at Florida State and still ranks third among all-time touchdown passes in FSU history with 57. "Coach made tough decisions off the field. He was willing to give players second chances if they were willing to prove themselves. Randy Moss was a perfect example. He was headed to Notre Dame to play for Lou Holtz but he got in some trouble and Notre Dame couldn't take him. Coach Bowden let Randy come to FSU and it didn't work out, but many players did get a college education because Coach was willing to take a chance on them."

Bowden made it pretty simple according to Clifton Abraham, who was one of four consecutive consensus All-America cornerbacks at Florida State, "He'd tell us, 'Never go out there and do anything to embarrass the team, the University or your mama,' " said Abraham. "In other words, 'Stay out of trouble'!"

Florida State safety Brian McCray agreed. "I was one of those players who messed up and he gave me a second chance," said McCray.

"It was just part of who Coach Bowden was. He wanted players to get a college degree and have a chance in life through playing football. Coach would remain loyal to you as long as you got your act together and straightened up."

Boldness is something they say Bowden had even as a player. Bill Nunnelley covered Samford for the Birmingham newspaper as well as the Samford school paper. He recalls one particular instance when Bobby – the player – showed the quality: "Bobby was playing quarterback for Howard in a Homecoming game against Union College in 1951. Bobby Dailey, his teammate, recalled that Bobby had been watching Georgia Tech play, and decided to add some of Tech's "belly series" pitchouts to Howard's attack – in the huddle.

"Not only had Howard not practiced these plays, they weren't even in Coach Earl Gartman's playbook.

"The coach was getting a bit excited about that," Dailey said, "but it all worked out and just opened up the whole thing for us. That was just Bobby Bowden. He always had a great offensive mind."

FACING THE CONSEQUENCES

Established leaders who read this book will pause here and exclaim, "A HA!"

Babe Ruth said, "Never let the fear of striking out get in your way." Easy to say, but challenging to do. After all, you do have to walk back to the dugout after striking out. An executive does have to face his board after reporting poor earnings, and Bobby Bowden did have to walk into that locker room after losing by one point.

Let's go back to Bowden's first season at Florida State. You will remember that the Seminoles won exactly zero games the year before and they didn't start any better in the Bowden era losing to Memphis State 21-12 and getting pummeled by Miami 47-0. Just two games into his FSU career, Bowden put his foot down and placed his stamp on the program all in one fell swoop.

FSU was getting ready for No. 4 Oklahoma in Norman after that humiliating loss to the Hurricanes and Bowden knew he needed to do something. He called in six freshmen and promoted them to starting positions. "We had to change something," Bowden said in an interview during the 1980 season. "We just decided that if we were going to get whipped we had better get some of the younger players ready to go because they were the future."

Don't discount the boldness of that move. Bowden was literally risking his job with the move. Older players, no matter how poorly the team performs, generally expect to get the playing time. The fact that the new head coach made such a dramatic move sent shock waves through the program at a time when shock waves were probably all that could breathe any life into it. The Seminoles lost at OU (24-9), but won five of their last eight including the last three in a row.

Bobby Bowden won 316 games as a college head coach, but he also lost 97 and one stood out as the worst of all. Would it be the national title game loss to Florida, Tennessee or Oklahoma? No, just a regular season game in his first season at West Virginia that sticks with him to this day.

"I learned a lesson that day at Pitt in 1970 that I carried around with me the rest of my life," said Bowden. "I thought of it every single time that I felt like we had a game in hand and I think of it every time I hear about somebody running up the score."

Bowden took his first Mountaineer team up to hated-rival Pitt for this fateful game. West Virginia had beaten the Panthers three years in a row and the Pitt team in 1970 was not any better than its predecessors.

West Virginia was rolling at halftime up 27 points and Bowden decided he would switch to the running game to avoid running up the score which WVU had clearly done the previous year.

As you can probably guess, Pitt starting coming back in the game and eventually won 36-35 giving Bowden what he calls the "worst loss I had in coaching."

Accounts in the Morgantown papers suggested that West Virginia fans had to be restrained from going in the locker room after Bowden. A beating from crazy fans wouldn't have felt any worse than Bowden did looking in the faces of his distraught team.

"I should have kept the pressure on, I shouldn't have gotten conservative," said Bowden in numerous reports in the years following the game.

See the leadership lesson here. The old question in sports about whether it is easier when you are chasing towards No. 1 or trying to stay No. 1 is always answered the same way by anyone who has been No. 1. Fighting people off is tougher than climbing to the top. Motivation is certainly easier when you are the chaser. When you do get to the top – when your division is finally ranked as most productive, or when you're sales team wins the contest, Bowden's message to you is clear. Don't be conservative. Find a way to stay motivated and innovative. Do not let up on the reigns, don't stop throwing the ball.

Don't think that Bobby Bowden or any other leader is not bothered when decisions they make don't work out. Bowden, I'm told, didn't sleep much on nights following a Florida State loss and even this remarkably grounded man could get caught up in the drama of a loss.

Former Florida State Sports Information Director Wayne Hogan frequently tells the story of a loss by Florida State to a very good Pitt team in 1983.

FSU had kicked a field goal and appeared to have stolen the momentum with 8:34 left in the game and trailing just 17-16. Florida State dropped the Panther's kick return man at his own 12-yard line and the Seminole bench began to get excited. It was then that Pitt showed what ball control was all about. Running mostly behind all-world offensive tackle Bill Fralic, Pittsburgh ran off every second of the 8:29 that showed on the clock using 19 plays and managing six first downs on the time killing drive. FSU never even got the ball back.

Bowden and his staff were stunned after the game and the fact that Florida State only had the ball for 22 minutes the whole game had a lot to do with their blank expressions.

The long plane ride home obviously didn't clear the head coach's head because that's where Hogan's story gets funny. He recalled "This was an old airport in Tallahassee and everyone had to grab their bags on the ramp so everyone, team, coaches, cheerleaders, boosters were standing around waiting for their bags.

"There was a big parking lot with those concrete curbs at each space to make sure you didn't pull too far up. All of a sudden there is a huge commotion and you see these headlights coming straight from the back of the parking lot towards the terminal. By straight I mean not going on the road but coming right through the lot. Ka-bam, ka-bam, ka-bam is all you heard as the car is driving over one row of curbs after another and the headlights are jumping up and then down.

"When the car pulls up we realize it's Coach Bowden and there is a strong smell of gasoline. He gets out and gets his bags and starts to drive off. John Eason, our receivers coach, starts chasing after him and pounding on his window to get him to stop.

"He was still trying to figure out how in the world we didn't get a chance to win that game."

PEP TALK AT MICHIGAN

We can't have a book on Bobby Bowden and not look in on at least one of his pregame speeches.

In 1991, then No. 1 ranked Florida State would take on No. 3 Michigan in Ann Arbor. It was the kind of big game that the Seminoles seemed to be playing just about every other week, but even by big standards this one was BIG. It was the kind of game that TV and radio folks talked about throughout the summer.

Florida State had Casey Weldon and Amp Lee and Terrell Buckley and Edgar Bennett and Marvin Jones and Kirk Carruthers and many more stars. The Wolverines had eventual Heisman Trophy winner Desmond Howard and Elvis Grbac and Greg Skrepenak and Ricky Powers and Butkus winner Erick Anderson and Corwin Brown. You get the picture – it was a big game!

The Big House was stuffed to the gills for this one with media members literally hanging off the press box roof. It was a crystal clear day and just about perfect in every respect if you were a Seminole fan.

Bowden was supremely confident with a loaded team and a pocket full of trick plays that included the throwback pass I wrote about earlier and a fake field goal in his arsenal.

We talked to at least four players who were in that locker room and heard that pregame talk. None remembered every detail, but we put them all together to get the whole picture.

Florida State players came jamming into the visitor's locker room as the Wolverine cheerleaders were dragging out the familiar Michigan banner for their team to run through. It was not unusual for Bobby Bowden to have given his fiery speech the night before, but not this weekend at Michigan.

The players were as keyed up as they had ever been and their inspirational head coach started out with a subdued tone that surprised them. Here was his message: "Men, I know we usually defer to the second half if we win the coin toss. But I've told our captains that I want to take the ball if we get the chance today. We've studied Michigan all week and they've got that massive offensive line. Elvis Grbac is as good as they come at being efficient with the ball and they can really run. When they don't, they've got that dadgum Howard out there to catch everything."

Now, the FSU players were looking around the room like what in the heck is going on. Little did they know they were playing right into Bowden's hands.

He spun on his heels so his back was to the team and wondered aloud: "We are just not sure that we can get the ball away from them when they have it. We aren't sure how many chances we are going to get, so I feel like we better take the ball right away,"

He sort of let that last bit trail off then spun around and shouted, "Like heck we are!" I want you to go out there and show them what Florida State football is all about. I want you flying around the field like crazy. I want you to makes plays and we are going to give them everything we got. We've got every play in for this one and we're gonna call 'em all!"

I'm told he never even really finished the speech. The team just erupted and then raced out the door onto the field.

I guess you can predict the outcome. Buckley and Howard had a clash for the ages and on Michigan's very first play Buckley stepped in front of the Heisman winner and raced into the end zone with an interception. The Seminoles never slowed down all afternoon en route to a dizzying 51-31 romp that actually offended some of Michigan's regular media.

Leadership requires summoning both competence and boldness to make the tough decision. Bobby Bowden was a master at both.

Chapter Seven:

CAN I GET YOU SOMETHING?

"I've learned a big fact of life over my coaching. God doesn't want your ability, he wants your availability. He needs people who will say, 'What do you want me to do?' "

—BOBBY BOWDEN

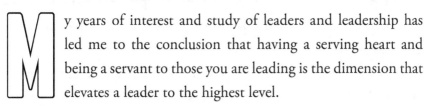 y years of interest and study of leaders and leadership has led me to the conclusion that having a serving heart and being a servant to those you are leading is the dimension that elevates a leader to the highest level.

Serving leaders understand that their achievements don't give them the right to push others around, or obliterate their competition, or decimate their rival congregation. Serving leaders realize that now that they have reached the top of their field, it is incumbent upon them to serve others with a heart filled with love and compassion.

A leader who is willing to serve finds himself standing shoulder to shoulder with the likes of Jesus, Gandhi, Mandela, Albert Schweitzer, Mother Teresa, Billy Graham, Martin Luther King, and a Bobby Bowden. It's a select field, but I invite you to join.

I use the analogy when I am speaking that you start out your leadership life with a bib as your first piece of equipment. The bib might as well be embroidered with the words, "It's all about me." We have seen leaders who have grown up and never taken that bib off. It's still all about them.

However, when a leader takes the next step and pulls off that bib and puts on an apron with the words, "Shaped to Serve," she moves on to the point where really exciting things can happen.

I learned all about Bear Bryant's serving heart when Tommy Ford and I researched him for my last book. He had this rough, tough exterior, but inside was a compassionate man.

I have been overwhelmed, simply overwhelmed, by the servant attitude that Bobby Bowden has displayed for more than 60 years. He took off that bib and put on an apron long ago.

Sue Semrau has coached Florida State's women's basketball team for the past 14 years and has taken seven straight teams to the NCAA Tournament. She enjoyed a particularly close relationship with Bobby Bowden at FSU.

"It was never about Bobby Bowden, it was always about everyone else first," said Semrau. "He was always concerned about putting other people in a position to be successful. That approach is biblically based – when you serve others you will reap the most. Coach Bowden was a leader who gave of himself.

"I had a player who passed away here at Florida State. Coach had had the same experience earlier. He sought me out and we cried together and he helped me through that tough period. That meant so much to me as a young leader. Now I try to reach out and do the same thing to other young leaders."

We should all take a lesson from the way Coach Bowden has treated Ann during over 60 years of marriage. She surely sacrificed a lot of personal goals and dreams to raise the Bowden clan and let Bobby earn the paycheck. He would be the last to tell you, but Bobby has been devoted to Ann over the years. How many of us would be devoted enough to have this story told of us.

David Benn was a linebacker at West Virginia from 1967-70. But now he is a painter who "paints beauty wherever I go," he told me. He went on to say, "I told Coach I wanted to do a painting for him and to mail me a photo that he thought captured real beauty," Benn said. "He sent me a photo of Ann and asked me to do her portrait. I was happy to do that for Coach, but the best part was the note he sent back. He wrote, 'This work you did of Ann will live for the life of my family.' That note meant the world to me."

West Virginia's Dan Wilfong said of Bowden, "Bobby's approach to life is 'Be the blessing, don't wait to be blessed.'"

West Virginia offensive tackle Dan Larcamp remembered Bowden as much for his off the field concerns as his coach. "Coach cared about his boys regardless of their performance on the field," he said. "He was concerned about his players as individuals. Their progress in school and development as young men was important to him."

Cory Niblock played offensive guard at FSU from 2003-2006 and Bowden clearly made a lasting impression on him. "Coach led by example and the foundation of his life was to do the right thing," he said. "In my life as a leader that is what I try to do even when no one is watching." And it is remarkable how Tom Florence, who played at West Virginia from 1976-78, had the identical quote. "Coach was a man of strong character who led by example," he said. "He practiced what he preached and that's why we listened to him and hung on every word."

Sammie Smith ran for 2,539 yards, which still ranks among FSU's top five all-time leading rushers, from his tailback position from 1985-88. He gave a first-hand account of the servant in Bobby Bowden.

"Coach Bowden was a stand-up guy, a father-figure type," said Smith. "He taught me that when you face hurdles, you pick yourself up, dust yourself off and keep going. I made some bad decisions in life that were out of character for me. I never should've done those things. Coach Bowden showed understanding towards me. He stood by me when I was in Federal Prison. In June of 2010, he personally spoke in front of the governor to attest to my character so I could have my civil rights restored. As far as I'm concerned with Coach Bowden, it's not about football."

All-America center Clay Shiver saw his coach's compassion when he played at Florida State in the early 1990s. He told me, "Coach never wavered with his compassion to develop the young men under his care. When he recruited a player in the kid's living room, he made it clear to the parents that he had a four or five year stewardship with their boy. He would tell the boy's mom that her son would go to class, get a degree and go to church at least twice a year, once at a predominately black church and one mainly white."

Nancy Andrews is the wife of former West Virginia player Carl Andrews, "Carl and I were dating at college," she said. "We didn't have a car, so one day we're walking along this narrow country road. A car screeched to a halt next to us. It was Coach Bowden who invited us to get in the back seat. He just said, 'Can I carry you somewhere?' After we got in and took off, Coach was turning around talking to Carl on this little tiny road and swerving like crazy. I was never so scared in my life.

"Coach came to our wedding just two weeks before two-a-days and I'm sure he had more important things to do. When Carl's mother died of cancer, Coach Bowden was at her funeral. He was always looking out for his players."

Everette Brown was a star defensive end for Florida State from 2006-2008 and is now a member of the Carolina Panthers. "One year we were having a rough season and the media was coming down hard on Coach," Brown said. "We had finished a long tough practice and were walking to the locker room when I look up and saw two college girls who recognized Coach Bowden. They were so excited to see him as they ran over to him. He stopped and spent ten minutes talking with them and took a picture. He took the time to make those young ladies feel special. Coach didn't suddenly come alive when the cameras were on. That's why we all respected him so much."

Gene Deckerhoff has been the voice of the Florida State Seminoles since 1979 (Bowden's fourth season) and is a 12-time winner of Florida's Sportscaster of the Year. He has also been the Tampa Bay Buccaneers play-by-play voice for the past 22 years.

In order for Deckerhoff, who is also one of Bowden's closest friends, to make the Bucs NFL games every Sunday he had to tape the *Bobby Bowden TV Show* right after the games and then catch the first flight out the next morning or climb into his motor home and drive to Tampa if it was a home game.

On the surface that may not sound like that big of a deal but how about when FSU is on the road at Boston College and Tampa Bay is playing the next day in San Francisco?

The opportunity with the Bucs was remarkable but Gene would have to approach Coach Bowden about taping the show whenever they got home. For road games at Boston College, or Maryland, or Syracuse or Nebraska that meant that the two would climb off the FSU charter as late as 4:00 a.m. and go on television to talk about a game that neither had even been able to review.

"Coach never hesitated for a second," said Deckerhoff. "He said, 'Gene, this is just too good an opportunity for you and I don't want to do the show with anyone else. Let's just do what we need to.' How many coaches would do that for someone?"

Tamarick Vanover was one of the Seminoles all-time great kickoff return men. "Coach established a fatherly role and it made you wish he was your daddy," he said. "In fact, he was a father to all those kids he coached over the years; a parent away from home. One time I had an incident with Coach Bowden where I was in trouble. He just told me straight out that, 'If you were my son, I wouldn't let you get away with that.' To be honest, I thought it was pretty cool that he would treat it so personally."

Garrett Ford was one of the first black players at West Virginia. He said, "I was just an 18-year old kid and Coach Bowden invited me to his home for dinner. Terry and Tommy were just little kids at the time. I had never even been in a white family's house, so that was a big event in my life."

Listen to this story just pour from a former player's heart.

"I went to FSU late after deciding not to attend the Air Force Academy, which meant no scholarship at the start of my career at FSU," said Marty Riggs who was the deep snapper in the mid 1980s. "After my junior year, I was having a really difficult time across the board. I had come to the end of my rope when I ventured over to Coach's office. He could see I was near tears, so he asked Sue Hall to hold all his calls. We sat in there for over two hours. Coach told me to talk to him, 'Like, I'm your Daddy.' Basically, Coach talked me off the ledge. He medicated my heart that day and put a bandage on it."

Dave Jagdmann played tight end at West Virginia from 1970-74. He told me, "Coach Bowden always had time for you and he never forgot his players. Twenty years after he left West Virginia and went

CAN I GET YOU SOMETHING?

to FSU, my son was diagnosed with cancer. Coach had all the Florida State players sign a ball and sent it to my son. Not many head coaches would think of doing something like that. If you could live your life like Bobby Bowden did, you'd be doing pretty darn good."

"Coach was great at responding in situations that were stressful and he did it with compassion," said Forrest Connoly, who played offensive tackle in the early 1990s. "The Foot Locker incident (several FSU players were found to have taken sneakers and sweat shirts purchased by a sports agent in violation of NCAA rules) was a perfect example. I never went in that store. At 6-7, 350 pounds and a size 17 shoe, what could I fit in at Foot Locker? The whole thing came to a head and I got suspended for more games than anyone else. Through all of this, Coach kept me afloat. He didn't look down on me and blame me for harming the FSU program which he built, which made me feel good about playing for him. The mark of a great leader is how they handle situations when the chips are down. The approach Coach used was to take your mistakes, learn from them and move forward. Throughout that Foot Locker issue, Coach told me, 'If you did it, tell the truth, take your punishment and be back when you can.' I used that whole incident from years ago to instruct kids today about doing the right thing."

Tony Bryant played defensive tackle in the NFL for seven years, but before that he played for Bowden at Florida State. He said, "I had a big adjustment to make when I came to FSU because I was coming from a junior college. Coach met with me personally and told me I could not just hang out. He was really kicking me in the tail. He said that I had to go to class and really study hard. Then he asked about my family and said to make sure everything at home was good. 'Do what you have to do to make it good,' he said. He was concerned with my specific problems and wanted to help me any way he could."

FSU linebacker Travis Sherman remembered when Bowden first visited his home. "Coach walked through the door and saw my Dad was barefooted," remembers Sherman. "He just took his shoes off and came right in and made himself at home. That's who coach Bowden was, a father figure to all of us. He cared about his boys and drove three key lessons home to us: 1. Do the right thing 2. Be the right person 3. Love life."

Sue Hall talked about the fact that Bobby Bowden would always write back whenever he would get a letter. "You would not believe the stack of mail that would come in some times," she said laughing. "I would pull out anything business related and sort of manage that on his calendar, but he insisted on reading anything of a personal nature himself. He would dictate letters to me on the business side, but he would usually hand write tons of letters back to people on other things."

Bowden never turned down a chance to serve his fellow man. He spoke from every pulpit he could find, still does, and helped inspire and reassure literally hundreds of thousands of people over the years.

Rob Wilson told me that a friend of his called out of the blue one day and said he had gone to the funeral of an acquaintance at work. He told him that at the church they had a number of photos and memories of the deceased. Among those articles was a framed, hand-written letter from Bobby Bowden. Rob's friend went on to say that it wasn't just some generic letter about having courage and hope, he said it was very compassionate and personal. Everyone at the service was moved by it.

Bowden probably wrote thousands of those letters over his coaching career and he did so with a willing heart.

Alabama head coach Nick Saban would have you know that Bowden often went far beyond just writing letters.

Two years ago, Saban told a packed Birmingham, Alabama banquet hall a story about Bowden. Saban was being presented the Coach of the Year trophy by the Birmingham Touchdown Club which had named the trophy in Bowden's honor. Little did they know how appropriate it would prove in that first year.

Saban recounted that he grew up in West Virginia not too far from Morgantown. His father passed away and he was busy coaching as a graduate assistant at Kent State at the time. He said his phone rang and it was West Virginia head coach Bobby Bowden on the line. "Coach said he knew that I might have family obligations with the death of my father," said Saban. "He went on to tell me that he would have a place for me on his staff at West Virginia if I felt like it would be better to be close to home during this time. It was such a gracious and generous offer. I will always remember what that offer meant to me."

WISDOM YOU CAN MAKE WORK

I'm told by my grandchildren that *Professor Dumbledore* from the *Harry Potter* series is their generation's poster child for Wisdom.

My generation had different role models for that virtue and I am sure you probably do as well. I would suggest that the thoughts shared by those that Bowden touched in the next few pages on his caring nature and lasting influence speak as much to his wisdom as anything else.

"He met all his players where they were," said former FSU and Atlanta Falcons linebacker Henri Crockett. "We were not all the same and he knew that. His conversation with me may be totally different than the one with Derrick Brooks, even though the subject was the same. Coach would be up in that tower always trying to figure out what made each guy tick. Coach Bowden would say, 'You aren't all the same and I'll treat you all differently. I'll deal with you where you are, so let's do what we have to do to make you better. We have one common goal, so let's play for the same cause.'"

Terrell Buckley, the 1991 Jim Thorpe Trophy winner and an NFL veteran of 14 years, said, "Coach Bowden was consistent in everything – his faith, his life, his rules, his practices." He had one rule that I really liked, 'However you are going to play in a game, however you're going to act, you need to do it in practice. If you do it in practice, you can do it in a game.' Coach was the same guy every day. You need to see a leader do that and not all of them have it."

Harvey Clayton played for Florida State from 1980-83. He said, "Coach gave us all the support he could to give us a chance to succeed. Coach would not give up on you and believed in giving guys a second chance because he always believed in his players. The guys he helped would be called into his office, talked to and then nurtured. Usually they would go on to better things in life."

Richie Andrews was a Seminole kicker from 1987-90. "Coach has visited a million homes and eaten that much chocolate pie," Andrews said. "But he remembers everyone. To this day he'll see me and say, 'Hey Buddy, how's your mom and dad.' He really cared about you and your family."

Bowden's wisdom in dealing not only with his players, but their families as well dates way back in his career.

"I get emotional when I talk about Coach Bowden and I want you to know why," West Virginia's John Harcharic told me. "Coach Bowden made people feel special and for me it had to do with my parents. As background, my parents were everyday, middle-class, working people from a small steel mill town in northern West Virginia. My mother was a school teacher at my Catholic grade school and my father was a foreman in the tin mill. They were relative 'nobodies.' They stressed my education above all and didn't even want me to play football in high school. Therefore, I was always a good student, even through college, where I completed my first two years of Pharmacy School while playing football at WVU.

"My parents always told me about when they would come down on the field after home-games to meet me and Coach Bowden would see them. They told me how he would go out of his way to come over to them and thank them for doing such a good job in raising me. I can't tell you how special that made them feel! You could see them just beaming with pride in themselves, and their son.

"That is why I get emotional when I speak about Bobby Bowden to anyone. I can never say enough good things about Coach for many, many reasons, but that one thing alone about my parents is enough for me."

Mike Bianchi is the lead sports columnist for the *Orlando Sentinel* and has written some of the most critical columns on Bobby Bowden. At the same time he has written on more than one occasion that he thinks Bowden was the finest coach in college football history. I was anxious to hear what he had to say.

"Bobby always had a knack of making anybody and everybody – fans, reporters, high school coaches and even the last walk-on at the end of his bench, feel like they were important," Bianchi said. "From a media standpoint, Bobby was always accessible and accommodating and treated your profession with respect. He always believed that if he treated people with respect, he would get that in return. For the most part, I believe he did. I think his first national title – when the voters put him in the championship game despite a late-season loss to Notre Dame – can be at least partly attributed to Bobby's likeability. In a buttoned-down profession filled with paranoid, control-freak coaches who lock down their programs like a gulag, Bobby always took great pride in keeping his program open and friendly. It's this sort of attitude that attracted recruits, won over their parents and allowed him to build one of the most awesome and amiable dynasties in college football history."

What a testament to wisdom, but it doesn't stop there.

Walter Barnes was Bowden's assistant coach way back at Howard College in 1959. He said, "Bobby cared about his players. If a boy got in trouble, he'd give him a second chance. He would bring the boy in, give him a talking to and tell it like it was. The boy must straighten up and if he didn't he would be on the road."

Thirty years later, Shannon Baker played wide receiver for Bowden at FSU. He said, "Coach cared about you. He truly cared about my life and that won me over. I came from a single parent home and Coach became a male figure who was committed to me. He cared about the outcome of my life which made me want to knock myself out for him. I didn't want to disappoint him. He made you want to join his team and then rally for him. That has carried over for me in trying to help young men today."

Former FSU sports medicine director Randy Oravetz appreciated Bowden's methods. "He loved to have the kids around him," said Oravetz. "He'd get on the players when needed but he'd laugh and say, 'You probably don't think I was ever 20, but I was and at 20 I probably did some of the same things you did.' He was good at joshing around with the players, but he was so smart with how he would get his point across."

"I liked the way he would end a conversation with you by saying, 'Dadgumit son,'" said Ken Oslegar who played tight end from 1967-71. "It made you feel as if you were his son and part of the Bowden team. He made you feel part of the group whether you were a star or a bench-warmer.

"Playing football for Coach helped me with discipline in my life. You had to make a commitment to football, your studies, the training table, off-season workouts, etc. That has carried over to the whole course of my life development."

Even back in those early days at West Virginia you could see Coach had the tools to be a great coach. He was very well-liked because we all knew he'd stand beside you to protect you."

Scott Hinley, who played at West Virginia from 1968-71, called Bobby Bowden the "fairest man I've even met. If you gave coach 100% he was in your corner," he said. "He treated all of us equally and liked us for who we were."

I am not sure you can even measure the value of having someone in a leadership role who inspires those kind of thoughts from people he had working for him. As I was scribbling down these quotes and the ones that follow, I kept getting a mental picture of the great military leaders who had to send their "boys" into combat and yet they came out of it with nothing but admiration for their leader.

Rick Weiskirsher took what he learned playing cornerback at West Virginia from 1969-73 into his professional life. He said, "I coached high school football for 35 years and followed the Bowden philosophy. You need to care for your players and they will care about you," he told me.

Travis Johnson played defensive tackle at FSU and in the NFL. "After I graduated and was waiting for the draft, Coach came up to me and asked how my sister was doing." said Johnson. "He met my sister five years earlier when he was in our house recruiting me. You respect something like that. There are all sorts of different people at FSU, but Coach remembered about you and your family."

Zack Crockett played 12 years in the NFL at fullback. He said, "I still use Coach's message today. It was, 'Start it, Finish it. Give it your all. Lay it all on the line and don't leave anything on the field.' He taught us to be a bully out on the field, but be a classy bully. Act like a professional. We pushed each other every day, but at the end of the day we were a family."

Bob Gresham was a running back at West Virginia from 1967-70 and left with something he cherishes to this day. "Coach wanted all his players to get a college degree," he said. "He made sure we all had tutors if we needed them. Coach's main concern was that we did well in school. When he recruited me, he promised me I'd get my degree. I became the first member of my family to graduate from college. He taught me more about life than he did about football. That's what a good leader does."

Chris Davis was an electric high school quarterback who everyone wanted. He made his mark at wide receiver for FSU from 2003-2006 and is still playing in the NFL. He spelled out the Bowden wisdom pretty succinctly. "It was great to see how he handled and worked with all of us," said Davis. "Here's how I saw it: 1. He disciplined us like we were his children. 2. He spoke to us like a father. 3. We always knew what he stood for because he carried himself the same every day.

"So many players went to FSU because of Bobby Bowden. I know it played a big part in my decision. You can't think of Florida State without thinking of Bobby Bowden."

A DEVOUT START TO THE DAY

Let's take a time out here to look a little closer at what was a fundamental part of the Bobby Bowden way, and that was his practice of starting every day and every staff meeting with a devotional.

"I just always believed that everyone needs help, everyone needs guidance," said Bowden to the Panama City First Baptist Church in 2010. "Why not start your day by asking the very best source for help and inspiration?

"I think that being able to speak to God directly is one of the greatest and most important gifts that he has given us," said Bowden. "I'm sure not all of my coaches enjoyed being a part of that, but being exposed to it sure didn't hurt them any."

I pointed out earlier in the book about the ESPN image of Bobby Bowden sitting at his kitchen table in a bathrobe reading his Bible and praying. The idea of going to God in prayer to start your day, or a staff meeting, has its roots in colonial times. The story is worth telling considering it comes from an address made by Benjamin Franklin to the Continental Congress:

Mr. President:

The small progress we have made after four or five weeks close attendance & continual reasoning's with each other – our different sentiments on almost every question, several of the last producing as many noes as ays, is methinks a melancholy proof of the imperfection of the Human Understanding. We indeed seem to feel our own wont of political wisdom, since we have been running about in search of it. We have gone back to ancient history for models of government, and examined the different forms of those Republics which having been formed with the seeds of their own dissolution now no longer exist. And we have viewed Modern States all round Europe, but find none of their Constitutions suitable to our circumstances.

In this situation of this Assembly groping as it were in the dark to find political truth, and scarce able to distinguish it when to us, how has it happened, Sir, that we have not hitherto once thought of humbly applying to the Father of lights to illuminate our understandings? In the beginning of the contest with G.

Britain, when we were sensible of danger we had daily prayer in this room for the Divine Protection. Our prayers, Sir, were heard, and they were graciously answered. All of us who were engaged in the struggle must have observed frequent instances of Superintending providence in our favor. To that kind providence we owe this happy opportunity of consulting in peace on the means of establishing our future national felicity. And have we now forgotten that powerful friend? Or do we imagine that we no longer need His assistance?

I have lived, Sir, a long time and the longer I live, the more convincing proofs I see of this truth – that God governs in the affairs of men. And if a sparrow cannot fall to the ground without his notice, is it probable that an empire can rise without his aid? We have been assured, Sir, in the sacred writings that "except the Lord build they labor in vain that build it." I firmly believe this; and I also believe that without his concurring aid we shall succeed in this political building no better than the Builders of Babel: We shall be divided by our little partial local interests; our projects will be confounded, and we ourselves shall be become a reproach and a bye word down to future age. And what is worse, mankind may hereafter this unfortunate instance, despair of establishing Governments by Human Wisdom, and leave it to chance, war, and conquest.

I therefore beg leave to move – that henceforth prayers imploring the assistance of Heaven, and its blessings on our deliberations, be held in this Assembly every morning before we proceed to business, and that one or more of the Clergy of this City be requested to officiate in that service.

Dr. Magdi El Shaway played offensive line at Florida State in 1987 and 1988 before an injury cut his career short. He is now in the administration of the athletics department at USC. "His Christian principles anchored his approach to leadership," said El Shaway. "What Coach was on the inside, he was on the outside as well. Coach would talk to us about life values and life principles. He was a man of principle and wanted us to grow up and be like that as well. The two key words Bobby Bowden drilled into us were behavior and character."

Darnell Dockett is currently one of the NFL's top defensive linemen for the Arizona Cardinals and clearly a big fan of his former Seminole head coach. "He was a good person, very understanding because he was a player's coach," said Dockett. "When I was at FSU he put me in a position where I could succeed and gave me an opportunity to build a career I didn't even think I could ever have."

Joe Kines, who coached with Bowden late in his FSU career, gave thoughts on him that read like a road map of wisdom in action. "Bobby knew who he was and what his life's purpose was and thus he was very comfortable with himself," said Kines who coached linebackers. "Coach Bowden never worried about his decisions because he was so well grounded in faith. He was at peace with himself and the stress of coaching. Therefore, nothing was a crisis to him, just the next event. Bobby's view was that if he lost a great player, it was just an opportunity for someone else to step up and do something great. The players never saw Coach sweating or wringing his hands in despair. If they had, that would've had a negative impact on their outlook."

Paul McGowan, the 1987 Butkus Award winning linebacker, has an awfully good take away from his experience with Bobby Bowden. "As an adult leader, I hear Coach Bowden's voice in my head today," he said. "He's saying, 'Be a good person and the rest will fall into place.' "

Green Bay Packer fans remember Edgar Bennett for his seven years as a player for the team. (He is now on the coaching staff.) Florida State fans remember him as one of their all-time favorites from 1987-91. Bennett himself remembers Bowden this way: "As a communicator, Coach knew how to reach his players," said Bennett. "He respected us and we respected him. He was genuine and trustworthy. My family and I saw that when he recruited me and nothing changed after I got to FSU. He remained the exact same person and never shocked us with erratic behavior. He was strong in his Christian beliefs. They were a rock for him and formed the foundation of his philosophy as a leader. Coach remained true to his beliefs and never tried to be someone he wasn't. During times of crisis, Coach stayed steady and poised and all of his players noticed that."

BOWDEN'S DIRECT MESSAGE ON LEADERSHIP

As I mentioned before, Bobby and his son Steve released a book in 2001 called *The Bowden Way* and it is an outstanding self-examination of how he perceives leaders should act. Bobby was interested in the concept of this book which examines his leadership skills from those who followed him. However, we would be remiss if we didn't point out this particularly pertinent message from *The Bowden Way*.

Bowden talks about the death of one of his players, Devaughn Darling, during an off-season Florida State conditioning drill as one of the most difficult events of his coaching career. He included the message that Seminole linebacker Brian Allen delivered at the on-campus memorial:

> *It makes no sense that D.D. would be here one moment and gone the next. It makes no sense that at one moment he's a big strong football player and the next moment he'll never play*

football again. But reality isn't always what we want it to be, or what we think it should be. Reality isn't fair, it's just what it is. Bad stuff happens to good people.

"Bad things happen to good people," Bowden repeats in his book.

"We can all recite that mantra easily enough," he continues. "And we observe it more than we'd like. Bad things sometimes happen to good people. Good things sometime happen to bad people.

"If you wish to be a great leader, then accept down deep inside yourself that life is not fair," wrote Bowden. "You are not owed a great hand to play. But you are given an opportunity, and the strength, to face an adversity that arises."

Then he cautions, "Adversity will come and you will face it. A good leader will offer others a path worth following."

He has certainly provided that for me and I hope for you.

Ken Alexander roamed the middle linebacker position for the Seminoles, including leading the 1993 national championship team in tackles. He has gone on to become a successful lawyer in Tallahassee.

"Coach Bowden was the ultimate leaders' leader," he said. "He was a dad to the players because he gave us a male role model. He was an uncle to his coaches, a grandfather to the university, and to the recruits, he was mama's best friend."

In short, the total leadership package.

EPILOGUE

Wayne Atcheson is the former Sports Information Director at the University of Alabama and the first Director of the Billy Graham Library in Charlotte, North Carolina.

He refers to Bobby Bowden as my "good friend and much like family."

Wayne's brief essay on Bobby Bowden as a leader captures beautifully and succinctly everything we've been writing for the past seven chapters.

I believe Coach Bowden is among the fifteen percent of leaders who are born and not made. He was a college head coach at 25, and was only 30 when I first knew him as an 18-year-old freshman at Howard College serving as his sports publicity guy. I remember his sons Tommy (6) and Terry (4) clicking behind his heels on the practice field.

He was packed with energy like a locomotive and his personality beamed like a Ronald Reagan movie star. He was young but that was a plus to this charming man with good looks, and one that never appeared to walk but was always running and leading. And everybody behind him enjoyed trying to keep up with him.

At this stage, he was probably still as good as anyone on the team and we had some good athletes. As August practices began, this young general works his boys hard, the Bear Bryant way. The boys knew he was going to take them to eight or nine wins and would beat teams like Chattanooga and Furman who played major college teams.

With only two assistants, Coach Bowden's staff of three had these boys working as a machine on defense and offense. The kicking game was good and the young coach had burners returning kicks. Coach Bowden's brand of ball was fun and exciting from the beginning and his reservoir of leadership led to wins 80 percent of the time. Winning big was the object. Losing was for the other side.

Nehemiah might have been thinking of Bobby Bowden when he wrote, "The joy of the Lord is in your strength," in Chapter 8, verse 10. His leadership reflected the job of a highly spirited man. He was winsome, he was happy; he was loose and full of pep always. His energy level inspired confidence and winning was just expected and resulted.

I believe that maintaining his youth and energy with his smile, southern folksy charm, his "dadgum" statements and "Hello ole buddy, How 'ya doin" slaps on the back caught on with the fans and media, and especially the boys. He recruited the mommas and daddies. He was an RC Cola, Moon Pie kind of guy. All of this endeared him to make the game of football fun.

His youth, energy, enthusiasm and motivation attracted players to him. He wasn't mean at all, but tough, yes. I believe he would have been a winner at any college that was committed to a winning program.

Coach Bowden was blessed to be born in East Lake in Birmingham. He lived in the same neighborhood as the great Harry Gilmer, one of Alabama's finest. Harry was just three and a half years older than Bobby who idolized his neighbor. Bobby lived around players who went on to play for Alabama, the school he loved dearly, and its traditions impacted him. The love of the game was ingrained and it has not left him to this day. While he never coached at Alabama, it was Alabama that inspired him to greatness as a college coach. The standard of greatness he saw in Crimson Tide Rose Bowl and Sugar Bowl teams made an indelible impression. He took this blessing from God and never stopped running with it.

Coach Bowden never had to get religion. He had it when he was born to God-fearing parents growing up in Ruhama Baptist Church singing "What A Friend We Have In Jesus," "Amazing Grace," and "When The Roll Is Called Up Yonder," It was in his heart to stay. That old time religion was in his heart and soul on the sideline for all those victories. And he won those games without cussing on the field and still had time to teach a Sunday school class. If he worried and was tense on the sideline, it didn't show. He was full speed ahead on offense, pin your ears back on defense and go at it full throttle. That's where the trick plays came in. Somebody has got to win the game and it may as well be us.

His leadership technique of faith, fun, relax and enjoy football because after all it is just a game, is a recipe for any football coach who wants to be good and succeed. Coach Bowden smiled a lot and laughed a lot. His strength was in the joy of the Lord. His strong faith carried over and his coaching benefitted.

He delighted in doing what the Lord wanted (Psalm 1:2) out of him and he has become the envy of many and the standard for a football coach in terms of leading young men to be winners. As Coach Tom Landry once said, "Coaching football is getting a group of men to do what they don't want to do to accomplish what they've always wanted." Every player Coach Bowden had won. And it all began with him and who can deny that it was Bobby Bowden and his faith that made it so. His coaching idol was Bear Bryant and he would have been so proud and I know Harry Gilmer, his playing idol, is today. It has been one of the great joys of my life to follow his career since those Howard College days.

EXCERPTS FROM BOBBY BOWDEN'S NOTES TO HIS STAFF PRIOR TO HIS FINAL FLORIDA STATE SEASON IN 2009

Loyalty —Still Number One

*"If you listen to the fans, you're going to end up sitting next to them."
Marv Levy*

"If you want to lead the orchestra you must turn your back on the audience." Marv Levy

There is nothing more unjust than public opinion.

*When you are weak, you make others around you weak.
When you are strong others will draw on your strength.*

Don't hate adversity. Adversity will introduce you to your friends and enemies. It's always an opportunity.

The best way you can repay your players for making you a winner is to see that he gets his degree.

*Our staff must support and care for each other.
Key to squad morale; staff morale and being 'FAIR' – not equal.*

A confused player cannot be aggressive.

*Nothing in the world can take the place of Persistence. Talent will not; nothing is more common than unsuccessful people with talent.
Genius will not; unrewarded genius is almost a proverb.
Education will not; the world is full of educated derelicts.*

*Fear is the worst enemy of human personality.
Enthusiasm can cancel out fear.*

Fuss and argue about what we are going to do, but once we settle on a plan, we all pull together.
Anybody can coach a 3-hour practice.
A great coach can organize it in 1½ hours.

To most youth and some adults, peer approval is more important than self approval.

Don't depend on the undependable.

Strength does not come from winning your struggles, it comes when you decide not to surrender.

A winner says, "It may be difficult, but it is possible."
A loser says, "It may be possible but it is too difficult."

If you give all your players a test and they all fail it, whose fault is it?

"A person who knows 'how' will always have a good job.
The person who knows 'why' will always be his Boss!"

The mark of a good coach is how hard you get your players to play!

We have the talent, but talent only gives you a chance.

"Practice is 'preparation', not punishment." George Perles.

THE AUTHORS ACKNOWLEDGE AND
THANK ALL THOSE WHO CONTRIBUTED TO
Bobby Bowden on Leadership:

Clifton Abraham

Ernie Accorsi

Ken Alexander

Billy Allen

Clyde Allen

Chuck Amato

Greg Anderson

Carl Andrews

Mickey Andrews

Nancy Andrews

Richie Andrews

Terry Anthony

Bob Antion

Tim Antion

Enzo Armella

Wayne Atcheson

Shannon Baker

Bob Barrineau

Walter Barnes

Chad Bates

David Benn

Edgar Bennett

Louis Berry

Mike Bianchi

Furman Bisher

Harry Blake

Anquan Boldin

Monk Bonasorte

Bobby Bowden

Jeff Bowden

Terry Bowden

Tommy Bowden

Ken Braswell

Everette Brown

Lavon Brown

Tony Bryant

Terrell Buckley

Wally Burnham

Leland Byrd

Jimmie Callaway

Bill Capece

Byron Capers

Phil Carollo

Greg Carr

Pat Carter

David Castillo

Doug Charley

Sam Childers

Deondri Clark

Ed Clark

Harvey Clayton

Bubba Coker

Forrest Connoly

Beano Cook

Jim Cookman

Lee Corso

Sam Cowart

Henri Crockett

Zack Crockett

Jim Crosby

David Cutcliffe

Buster Davis

John Davis

Chris Davis

Lawrence Dawsey

Darnell Dockett

Dedrick Dodge

John Donaldson

Gene Deckerhoff

Daryl Dickey

Doug Dickey

Rich Duggan

Jamie Dukes

Mark Durham

Steve Early

John Eason

Magdi El Shaway

Mark Euopulos

Chip Ferguson

Joey Ferolito

Richard Findley

Elliott Finebloom

Jimbo Fisher

John Flath

Randy Flinchum

Tom Florence

Dan Footman

Garrett Ford

Dr. Eric Forsthoefel

Kevin Forsthoefel, Esq.

Matt Frier

Mickey Furfari

Steve Gabbard

Maryjane Gardner

Rock Gianola

Steve Gilmer

Jim Gladden

Fran Gleason

Billy Glenn

Lamar Glenn

Bob Goin

Lee Good III

Richard Goodman

Bob Gresham

Jim Grobe

Larry Guest

Letroy Guion

Gen. Franklin Hagenbeck

Odell Haggins

John Hale

Chris Hall

Kyler Hall

Sue Hall

John Harcharic

Dave Hart

Geno Hayes

Jimmy Hewitt

Scott Hindley

Wayne Hogan

Mickey Holden

Skip Holtz

Chris Hope

Dave Hudson

Rodney Hudson

Bobby Jackson

Keith Jackson

Dave Jagdmann

Jerry Johnson

Lonnie Johnson

Travis Johnson

Greg Jones

Keith Jones

Jon Jost

Brent Kallestad

Bob Kaminski

Danny Kanell

Terry Kettlewell

Joe Kines

Bernie Kirchner

Jerry Kutz

Dan Larcamp

Chris Leak

Ronald Lewis

John Lilly

Thomas Loadman

Gary Lombard

Paul Lumley

Rudy Maloy

Mike Martin

Ray Mashall

Martin Mayhew

Peter McConnell

Errol McCorvey

Brian McCray

Gene McDowell

Bryant McFadden

Paul McGowan

Toddrick McIntosh

Bill McKenzie

Danny McManus

Fred McMillan

Tiger McMillon

Hubert Mizell

Jarad Moon

David Morris

Scott Mottern

Dan Mowrey

Sean Muhammed

Brent Musburger

David Nebera

W.B. Newton

Cory Niblock

Ben Odom

Randy Oravetz

Tom Osborne

Joe Ostaszewski

Artie Owens

Mike Owens

David Palmer

Mike Parsons

Ed Pastilong

Willie Pauldo

Paul Piurowski

Bob Pitrolo

Ron Pobolish

Christian Ponder

Ed Pope

Kendyll Pope

Wayne Porter

Chris Potts

Jeff Purinton

Clint Purvis

Theon Rackley

Bill Ragans

Todd Rebol

Neil Reed

Tom Reidemore

Andy Reters

Jamal Reynolds

Bobby Rhodes

Mark Richt

Marty Riggs

Josh Robbins

Dickie Roberts

Dave Roberts

Myron Rolle

Bonwell Royal

Mark Ruckman

Deion Sanders

Brian Schmitz

Howard Schnellenberger

Brad Scott

Chris Sears

Sue Semrau

Billy Sexton

Tom Shaw

Travis Sherman

Mike Sherwood

Clay Shiver

Mike Shuman

Ernie Sims

Corey Simon

Billy Smith

Chuck Smith

Ernie Sims

Clay Singletary

Dave Snyder

Connell Spain

John Spiker

John Spraggins

Ryan Sprague

Jack Stanton

Rohn Stark

Kevin Steele

Rick Stockstill

Bennie Storey

John Swofford

Rick Stump

Bob Thomas

Shelton Thompson

Tarlos Thomas

Rick Trickett

Donna Turner

Dr. Rick Vaglienti

Dave Van Halanger

Tamarick Vanover

Terry Voithofer

Andre Wadsworth

Chuck Walsh

Charlie Ward

Terry Warren

Peter Warrick

Drew Weatherford

Chris Weinke

Rich Weiskirsher

Doc Weiss

Casey Weldon

TK Wetherell

Pat White

Dan Wilfong

Alphonso Williams

B.C. Williams

Brett Williams

Dayne Williams

Tom Williams

Ray Willis

Russ Wilson

Kamerion Wimbley

Don Yeager

Donnie Young

Mike "Zeke" Zakowsky

Bob Zitelli

ACKNOWLEDGEMENTS

With deep appreciation we acknowledge the support and guidance of the following people who helped make this book possible:

Special thanks to Alex Martins, Bob Vander Weide and Rich DeVos of the Orlando Magic.

Thanks also to my writing partner Rob Wilson for his superb contributions in shaping this manuscript.

Hats off to three dependable associates —my trusted and valuable colleague Andrew Herdliska, my creative consultant Ken Hussar, and my ace typist Fran Thomas.

Hearty thanks also go to my friends at Advantage Media Group. Thank you all for believing that we had something important to share and for providing the support and forum to say it. Special thanks to founder Adam Witty for your continued support and encouragement.

And finally, huge thanks and appreciation go to my wife, Ruth, and my supportive children and grandchildren. They are truly the backbone of my life.

—PAT WILLIAMS

ABOUT THE AUTHORS

PAT WILLIAMS (ORLANDO, FLORIDA) – Few people know leadership better than Orlando Magic co-founder Pat Williams. A sports executive for over 40 years, Williams has led more teams than most of his contemporaries combined. The former General Manager of the Orlando Magic, Philadelphia 76ers, Atlanta Hawks and Chicago Bulls, Williams is the prolific author of 12 books on leadership, most recently *Lincoln Speaks to Leaders* and *Bear Bryant on Leadership*. Williams is a highly-acclaimed professional speaker, having keynoted for dozens of Fortune 500 organizations and has appeared on hundreds of news programs including *Good Morning America* and *Fox and Friends*. Williams and his wife Ruth reside in Orlando and are parents to 19 children (14 adopted from third world countries).

ROB WILSON (TALLAHASSEE, FLORIDA) – Few people know Florida State University and the coaches and former players better than Rob Wilson. Wilson's involvement with Florida State's athletic program dates back to his undergraduate days at FSU from 1982-83 and he has been with FSU continually since 1987. In his professional career, Wilson has served the Seminoles as Assistant Sports Information Director, Sports Information Director, Assistant A.D. for Media Relations and currently is Associate Athletic Director for Public Affairs. Wilson began his college days as a wide receiver under Steve Sloan at Ole Miss in 1980. Wilson and his wife Sherrill have two sons Preston (15) and Parker (12).

You can contact Pat Williams at:

Pat Williams
c/o Orlando Magic
8701 Maitland Summit Boulevard
Orlando, FL 32810
(407) 916-2404
pwilliams@orlandomagic.com

Visit Pat Williams' website at:
www.PatWilliamsMotivate.com

If you would like to set up a speaking engagement for Pat Williams, please call Andrew Herdliska at 407-916-2401 or e-mail him at aherdliska@orlandomagic.com.

We would love to hear from you. Please send your comments about this book to Pat Williams at the above address or in care of our publisher at the address below. Thank you.

Adam Witty
Advantage Media Group
65 Gadsden Street
Charleston, SC 29401

Printed in the USA
CPSIA information can be obtained
at www.ICGtesting.com
JSHW061437181223
53960JS00005B/45

9 781599 322643